Teaching Budding Scientists

Teaching Budding Scientists

Fostering Scientific Inquiry with Diverse Learners in Grades 3–5

Pamela Fraser-Abder, Ph.D.
New York University

PEARSON

Boston Columbus Indianapolis New York San Francisco Upper Saddle River
Amsterdam Cape Town Dubai London Madrid Milan Munich Paris Montreal Toronto
Delhi Mexico City Sao Paulo Sydney Hong Kong Seoul Singapore Taipei Tokyo

Acquisitions Editor: Kelly Villella Canton
Editorial Assistant: Annalea Manalili
Vice President, Director of Marketing: Quinn Perkson
Marketing Manager: Danae April
Production Editor: Janet Domingo
Editorial Production Service: Kathy Smith
Composition Buyer: Linda Cox
Manufacturing Buyer: Megan Cochran
Electronic Composition: Schneck-DePippo Graphics
Interior Design: Deborah Schneck

For related titles and support materials, visit our online catalog at www.pearsonpd.com

Copyright © 2011 Pearson Education, Inc.

To obtain permission(s) to use material from this work, please submit a written request to Allyn and Bacon, Permissions Department, 501 Boylston Street, Boston, MA 02116 or fax your request to 617-671-2290.

Between the time website information is gathered and then published, it is not unusual for some sites to have closed. Also, the transcription of URLs can result in typographical errors. The publisher would appreciate notification where these errors occur so that they may be corrected in subsequent editions.

Printed in the United States of America

10 9 8 7 6 5 4 3 2 1   14 13 12 11 10

www.pearsonpd.com   ISBN-10: 0-205-56956-0
ISBN-13: 978-0-205-56956-4

To: Roxanne, Stacy, and Camilla,
who continue to amaze me with their unending
questions, curiosity, sense of adventure and
consistent search for truth and justice.

Contents

Chapter 1

Chapter 2

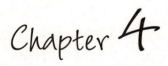

Chapter 3

Your Students and Science Learning   35

Chapter 4

Teaching and Learning Science Through Inquiry   49

Chapter 5

Exploring Process Skills with Your Students   67

Chapter 6

Establishing Your Science Program   89

Chapter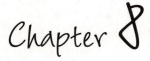

Chapter 8

Appendix 1

The National Science Education Standards and the Benchmarks for Science Literacy   137

Appendix 2

Science Content Information for Grades 3-5   153

Acknowledgments

I gratefully acknowledge the support of my colleagues Janice Koch, Robert Wallace, Jason Bloustein, Catherine Milne, Cecily Selby, and Marion Zachowski, who served as my support system as I began to envision the evolution and birth of this book, my students in the graduate elementary course, now New York City teachers: Audrey Elias, Lindsay MacPherson, Hallie Saltz, and Lindsey Webster, whose work appears in the book, and Kara Naidoo, doctoral student and urban teacher who reviewed the content in Appendix 2. Caitlyn Herman and Tammy Lam provided valuable research and editorial assistance, and my daughters Roxanne, Stacy, and Camilla Abder were always available for research, editorial, and technological assistance. The numerous reviewers who provided valuable and constructive criticism helped to create the final version of this book: Joe Alfano, Minneapolis Public Schools; Elizabeth Barrett-Alexander, Columbus Elementary School; Pamela Bowie Wheeler, Berea Elementary School; William D. Chang, Los Angeles Unified School District; Diana Keeney, Los Angeles Unified School District; Anita R. O'Neill, Montgomery County Public Schools; Beverly Ramsey, Bobby Ray Memorial Elementary School; John P. Skipworth, Huntsville City Schools; Jane Yuster, Alameda County Office of Education. I also acknowledge the thousands of teachers and teacher educators with whom I have worked both locally and globally. Much of what I have written here is a reflection of what I have learned from you in our discussions and workshop activities.

Thank you.

Foreword

Classrooms are busy places and the demands on elementary school teachers are greater than ever before. As you go about your school day, the challenge to create community in your classrooms, attend to the business of the school day, and organize the mandated lessons surrounding language arts and mathematics often leaves little time to help students learn about the natural world by doing science with them.

This book is a wonderful way to make friends with science and, as a classroom teacher, engage your students in experiences and experiments that examine enduring concepts in science and that will engage you in conversations with them about what worked and what didn't work.

As a science teacher educator, I have worked extensively with Pamela Fraser-Abder and I know that the topics and lessons she designed for the practicing teacher will help you feel excited and inspired about teaching science to young children.

This book will facilitate your own and your students' science learning. From classroom-based experiments to using the resources in your environment, the activities in this book will help you implement science in your own classroom. Doing science with children means you will engage them in their own experiences and in their own thinking. Young children will gain practice making observations, manipulating materials, gathering information, and discussing their ideas.

During the early years, our students are natural explorers. Be sure to use the suggestions in each chapter to help you encourage their quest to understand "why" things happen. While *inquiry* is a term often used in school science, be sure to examine just what we mean by inquiry when we engage children in science activities. Establishing a science program in grades 3–5 can be overwhelming. Be certain to use the suggestions in Chapter 6 to guide you in the development of your science curriculum.

Finally, use this book as a tool to help you and your young students have fun while learning about the natural world.

Janice Koch

Preface

Dear Teacher of Budding Scientists,

This book is written to assist you in developing, implementing, and evaluating your science teaching and your students' science learning. The research on science education equity and professional development that I have conducted for over two decades provides the foundation for this research-based, yet practical and friendly, professional development book. The title was chosen as a call to action to you, teachers of young students in grades 3–5, as you guide your students on their journey to scientific literacy, while fostering their interest and participation in science.

Students come to school with a constant need to investigate everything they encounter, but research shows that by the end of the third grade, this deep interest in science sometimes fades from lack of nurturing on the part of teachers, parents, and the community. Instead of losing interest in science, these third-graders should be "budding scientists" getting ready to blossom as future scientists as they move to secondary school. Our budding scientists will only achieve their potential if they receive a high-quality science education. And you hold the key.

As teachers, you play an important role in facilitating the learning process as your young students begin their journey to scientific literacy. To better explore your critical role in the development of budding scientists, I encourage you to reflect on the following questions throughout the book:

- What am I teaching?
- Who are my students?
- Why am I teaching science?
- How am I teaching science?
- How do I know that my students have learned science?

As you read this book, you need to wear two hats: that of a learner and that of a teacher. As you complete the activities in this book, you reflect on what you are doing and how you are learning. Then you learn to step back and view your experience as a teacher. What ideas did you struggle with? What helped you in the struggle? What ideas are your students likely to struggle with? How can you help them in their struggle? What strategies can you use to help them as they develop their own understanding?

Although some school districts' intense focus on literacy development has resulted in less attention to science teaching and learning, teachers will now be required to teach science in order to meet the mandates of the Science Accountability Act (H.R. 35). The act amends the No Child Left Behind Act of 2001 to require that science assessments are included in the state's accountability system by 2009. Given this new edict to teach science, you may feel daunted, confused, and maybe a little frightened. You might be asking yourself questions like: What do I need to know? What supplies do I need to purchase? Where can I find effective activities?

Some of you may be more comfortable with this new policy, if you already teach science and enjoy it. But other teachers may find it a challenge to make the transition from teaching little or no science to having to teach science that will be tested. This book is written to help you meet that challenge.

As you complete the reflections in the book, you should explore through your science autobiography and other reflection opportunities, your personal traits that determine the what, why, and how you teach; your deep-seated, often unconscious feelings toward science teaching and learning; your views on who has ownership of science. This approach to personal explora-tion is rooted in the context of schooling. Begin by exploring the following questions:

- What were your experiences with science as a student?
- What does it mean to teach science for all, and how do you teach for scientific literacy?
- What do you understand about how young students learn science?
- What are the implications of science in the daily lives of your students?

Begin to conceptualize science teaching as a personal activity requiring a large capacity for reflective thought and deliberate action and experimenta-tion. This book provides both knowledge about science content and process, curriculum, instruction, and pedagogy as well as a venue for personal exami-nation so that you may leave this professional development experience as a confident science teacher.

As you focus on teaching science, you will no doubt find numerous books about methods of teaching elementary science. My goal is not to recreate these books, but to share practical strategies with you and point you in the direction of potential activities and resources for use in your classroom and to help you expose your students to the informal world of science and to the surrounding community, which contains numerous, often free, resources for teaching science. Spend some time revisiting the experiences you had in your science methods courses and reviewing the texts you used then, as you engage in the activities in this book. The young students in your classroom are still filled with excitement and curiosity about nature. Let us use this enthusiasm to enhance their science learning. Many of the activities in this book deal with answering the questions your students might generate from interaction with their natural surroundings whether urban, suburban, or rural. Let us involve our young students in activities that they will always remember and build on as they move to the secondary school.

Our schools continue to cater to the needs of an increasingly diverse population. Diversity in learning styles and abilities, ethnicities, social class, religion, gender, culture, and language is represented in most of our schools. This book helps you to examine diversity in your classroom and determine how you can foster an effective learning community in your science classroom while being sensitive to the needs of all members of the class. Those of you who are teaching in the urban setting are well aware of the increasing diversity in your classrooms. For those of you teaching in suburban and rural settings, demographic changes are taking shape quickly. You will soon find yourself teaching an increasingly diverse student population. Do some in-depth reflection on who you are and who your students are. Before you can begin to teach science effectively, you need to understand yourself and your teaching philosophy. Then you need to begin to develop an understanding of your students. You cannot teach unless you know your audience. What are their views of science and scientists? What prior knowledge do they bring to your classroom? What are the demographics of the community in which you teach? What kind of support can you reasonably expect from parents and the community? What are the implications of the diversity in your class for how you develop and teach science lessons?

This book incorporates the following practical strategies for in-service teachers:

- tips for urban teachers
- classroom management tips for teachers conducting inquiry lessons
- suggestions for teaching science to English language learners and students with special needs
- ideas for connecting science and other content areas
- suggestions for using informal resources to teach science
- ideas for connecting your budding scientists with their local environment
- ideas for developing lessons based on the National/state science standards
- tips for creating assessments for inquiry-based lessons

Good science teaching and learning is a result of meaningful preparation and collaboration among teachers, students, parents, and the community. As a teacher, you have the power to make an outstanding contribution to the scientific pipeline by nurturing the critical thinking skills of budding scientists so they have the opportunity and foundation to become scientifically literate and our nation's future scientists. Through this text, my goal is to provide you with the information and prompts to help you evolve into an outstanding teacher of budding scientists.

This book is only a success if, by the end of the fifth grade, your students maintain their curiosity and deep interest in science, and continue to view science as a way of looking at and interacting with the world. Some of them will hopefully have begun to think about a future career in science.

Let's begin our journey to scientific literacy!

1

Factors That Influence Your Science Teaching Philosophy

Focus Questions

- Why teach science to young students?
- Who are you, and how do you feel about science?
- What are your views of science and scientists?
- Who are your students?
- How can you help your students succeed in science?

The increasing number of students from diverse cultures entering U.S. schools, combined with the national goal of scientific literacy for all students, creates a major dilemma for teachers who belong to cultures that are very different from the immigrant cultures. Current research literature suggests that students from different cultures bring alternative ways of knowing, communicating, and experiencing the world, which may be incompatible with the way science is traditionally defined, taught in our schools, and addressed in the state and national standards. This book begins by examining equity and access issues that have a major impact on science teaching and learning. During this in-depth investigation and reflection, you examine the following questions:

- Why teach science to young students?

- Who are you, and how do you feel about science teaching?

- Who are your students?

- What are their lives like?

- How can you help your students succeed in science?

Concurrent with this process of discovery about yourself and your often subconscious expectations for all students, you also engage in an in-depth examination and reflection on your students and their lived experiences. The final self-reflection leads you to examine the question:

- How does knowing who you are and who your students are make you a better teacher?

Once you come to a better understanding about who you are and what culturally embedded issues your students bring to the classroom, you can move on to dealing with your scientific self and examining your views of science and scientists.

Throughout this book, you will find many reflective activities and be guided to collect many resources. Keep your reflections or entries in this book or in a journal and file any research that you do online in a folder that you can use for reference in your curriculum planning and development.

Why Teach Science to Young Students?

Teacher Activity: Initial Reflection

List three reasons why you should teach science to students in grades 3 through 5.

1. _____

_____

_____

2. _____

_____

_____

3. _____

_____

_____

As we enter the era of global warming, decreased food supplies, and increased cost of energy, we become more aware of the importance of science and technology and the need to have our population capable of making decisions informed by scientific knowledge. At the same time, there is compelling evidence that only a small percentage of the students who pass through the school system develop any useful scientific literacy. We continue to produce graduates who lack even a basic understanding of science and technology, who have a negative attitude toward science, and who have not fully developed critical thinking skills capability. This paucity in science knowledge has increasingly unfortunate personal, social, and economic consequences, including the inability to take pleasure from the natural world, to make decisions that contribute to the sustainability of our environment, and to use science to inform decision-making processes. The increasing technological sophistication of the work place will require, at least, a basic knowledge and skill in science, mathematics, and technology.

Personal and civic decisions are often better made if guided by scientific knowledge. For example:

- When states propose shipping their garbage to other states or to remote areas in the state, can residents offer a better alternative?

- As new diet fads wax and wane, how do people sort out the competing claims and choose a safe method of losing weight?

- As the cost of gasoline rises each day and energy consumption becomes more and more of an economic issue, how do people respond? What knowledge do they use to guide their decisions?

Scientific understanding alone may not suffice to guide such decisions, but its absence will likely lead to poor solutions.

In the past, it was believed that only a handful of top students had the capacity to learn science while the remaining students—those who are average and especially those who are poor, female, or in a minority group—are widely assumed to be incapable of learning the math required in science, too concrete of mind to grasp scientific abstractions, or unwilling to endure the rigors of science education.

There is ample evidence, however, that the problem is not the child, but instead that science is not being taught or is often taught in a way that progressively diminishes students' interest in the subject and their confidence in their capacity to learn it. For many years, most elementary schools have taught only two subjects seriously—reading and mathematics—on the flawed assumption that this allows them to "leave no child behind."

Even where students are also taught science, the nature of the content and the way it is presented often fail to engage students' minds. Some elementary students are taught science as a series of fun experiments; others are offered "textbook" science, where they are taught facts and concepts but not given enough time and experience to connect those facts with the realities of the natural world or to grasp the underlying principles that make sense of it all. Thus, they quickly become bored by the seemingly pointless memorization of facts and terms. Not surprisingly, many students from all social classes and ethnic backgrounds decide that science is too boring and difficult. All children are capable of learning science and should have the opportunity to do so. Science provides them with a foundation for life as critical thinking adults who can contribute to the well-being of themselves and society.

When we consider the question "Why teach science?" it seems easy to answer in terms of the importance of science in society. We can immediately see the multitude of benefits from scientists' research and technologists' application in medicine, industry, transportation, agriculture, electronics, and technology. Think about what your day would be like if all of the scientific advances and applications that have been made in your lifetime alone were suddenly erased. How very different life would be without television, cell phones, or computers! You need to prepare your young students for a life full of technology, a type of life which has not yet been envisioned. You need to provide them with the skills to exist in that new world—a world in which critical thinkers and problem solvers will be the ones who survive and live successful lives.

The development of critical thinking skills has been emphasized as being of major importance if we want to produce rational thinkers and decision makers who can contribute to society. Great scientists are critical thinkers. The skills practiced by scientists help students become critical thinkers. Critical thinkers

- continually seek to know and to understand
- question all things
- interpret all available data
- base judgment on evidence
- respect logic
- consider consequences of their actions
- demonstrate intellectual independence

These critical life skills should be taught as part of science. For young students, their entire world is their laboratory; they continually seek to know, understand, and question all things. Though their efforts are often fumbling, students readily search for data and want verification. But what happens to their spirit of inquiry as they progress up the educational ladder? Why does the number of questions decrease? Perhaps part of the reason is a lack of opportunity to use scientific skills or thinking processes, so a decline in curiosity sets in.

There is no better way to help students satisfy their wanting to know, their questioning and searching, than to allow them to interact with objects and events of the natural world. This is what is involved in their doing science, why it is so important to them, and why you should make it important in your teaching. As a teacher of young students, your major role is to foster and encourage this questioning, this unending curiosity.

Teacher Activity: Reasons for Teaching Science

Now that you have read and reflected on the above, give five reasons why you think you should teach science to young students.

1. _____
   _____

2. _____
   _____

3. _____
   _____

4. _____
   _____

5. _____
   _____

Now that you have reflected on why you should teach science, let us turn to figuring out who you are and why you teach as you do.

Your Personal Context

Who Are You, and How Do You Feel about Science?

In a recent survey conducted as part of their classroom observation, some of my graduate students examined the status of elementary science teaching in the schools in which they were currently student teaching. Their results lend support to the belief that they do not need to teach science when they have their own elementary classroom. Their results showed that 40 percent of classes observed had a cluster teacher who was responsible for teaching one to two science sessions per week, 25 percent of classes had teachers who did one to three science sessions per week, and 35 percent of classrooms had no science instruction. These kinds of results indicate that many teachers may be struggling with understanding that the classroom teacher must teach science as an essential part of a well-rounded education that prepares students to be critical thinkers, problem solvers, and informed decision makers. These results mirror what is currently happening in elementary schools as teachers have mainly focused on mathematics and reading, the subjects that were being tested. However, with the recent introduction of science testing, there is more attempt to teach science in the classroom. To begin your journey of effective science teaching, you need to start with a clear idea as to where you position yourself in science teaching.

- What is the status of your current science teaching?
- Are you the classroom teacher who teaches science as part of your daily curriculum?
- Do you work closely with a cluster teacher, integrating what you do in other subjects with what is being covered in science?
- Do you leave all the science teaching up to the cluster teacher?

The answers to these questions will determine how much preparation you need to do to plan for teaching your budding scientist.

Teacher Activity: Initial Self-Reflection

Reflecting on the following questions will help you begin to focus on your science teaching. Be honest with your responses. No one will see your answers.

1. Can you recall what made you decide to teach young children?

2. What did you think of science then? Did you think it would be a difficult subject to teach?

3. How often are you teaching science now?

4. How are you teaching it? What strategies and resources do you use?

Based on your self-reflection, you might find that you fall into one of these categories:

- did not like science and do not teach it
- loved science and love teaching it
- teaching science because you enjoy teaching young students
- teaching science because you have to

Whatever category you fall into, the exercises in this book will help you develop into an effective teacher of young students. It is important that, as we begin to prepare for teaching science, you come to terms with your science teaching philosophy.

The best teachers are the ones who can respect and cultivate individual differences in their students.

What Is Your Teaching and Learning Style?

Here are some questions you may ask and respond to in order to construct a useful picture of yourself as a teacher.

Teacher Activity: What's Your Teaching and Learning Style?

1. Do I plan for what might happen in my class ahead of time, or would I rather cope with problems as they arise?

_____

_____

_____

2. Am I able to empower my students to do science even though I sometimes feel powerless myself?

_____

_____

_____

3. Am I a visual, auditory, naturalistic, or kinesthetic learner/teacher?

_____

_____

_____

𝒯eacher 𝒜ctivity: What's Your Teaching and Learning Style? (continued)

4. Under which of Gardner's learning styles (see Table 1.1) would I find myself described?

_____

_____

_____

5. Do I like objective testing tools made by an outside person, or would I rather rely on my classroom interaction to assess my children's learning?

_____

_____

_____

6. Do I use differentiated instruction in my class?

_____

_____

_____

7. Is my classroom teacher dominated or teacher facilitated?

_____

_____

_____

Howard Gardner, in his Theory of Multiple Intelligences, identified eight different types of intelligence: bodily-kinesthetic, interpersonal, linguistic, logical-mathematical, intrapersonal, spatial, musical, and naturalistic. Table 1.1 provides a brief description of each intelligence.

Gardner points out that, in this nation, education usually focuses primarily on linguistic and logical-mathematical intelligence. Intelligence is a mixture of several abilities that are all of great value in life. But nobody's good at them all. In life, we need people who collectively are good at different things. For further study, it is recommended that you read Gardner's books referenced at the end of this book. You could also visit Gardner's Website (http://www.usd.edu/trio/tut/ts/stylest.html) and take a quick test to determine your learning style.

Table 1.1 Gardner's Multiple Intelligences

Intelligence	Description
Bodily–kinesthetic	People are generally adept at physical activities (movement and doing) such as sports and often prefer activities that utilize movement.
Interpersonal	This area has to do with interactions with others. People in this category are usually extroverts and are characterized by their sensitivity to others' moods, feelings, temperaments, and motivations and their ability to cooperate in order to work as part of a group.
Linguistic	People with verbal-linguistic intelligence display a facility with words and languages.
Logical–mathematical	These individuals excel at reasoning capabilities, abstract pattern recognition, scientific thinking and investigation, and the ability to perform complex calculations.
Intrapersonal	Those who are strongest in this intelligence are typically introverts, self-reflective, and prefer to work alone. They are usually highly self-aware and capable of understanding their own emotions, goals, and motivations.
Spatial	People with strong visual-spatial intelligence are typically very good at visualizing and mentally manipulating objects. They have a strong visual memory and are often artistically inclined.
Musical	Those who have a high level of musical-rhythmic intelligence display greater sensitivity to sounds, rhythms, tones, and music. They normally have good pitch, and may even have absolute pitch, and are able to sing, play musical instruments, and compose music.
Naturalistic	This intelligence involves the ability to understand and work effectively in the natural world. This is exemplified by biologists and zoologists.

Teacher Activity: Reflection

This reflection provides you with some understanding of your teaching and learning style. It helps you to understand your mindset as you prepare for science teaching and interactions with your students. You need to understand yourself and your teaching style before you can begin to develop plans for teaching your students.

1. Where do you see yourself represented in Gardner's Learning Style Inventory?

_____
_____
_____

2. How does knowledge of Gardner's multiple intelligence help you in teaching science?

_____
_____
_____

3. What are the implications for how you teach science?

_____
_____
_____

4. How does it affect how your students learn science?

_____
_____
_____

5. How will it affect your teaching strategies and lesson planning?

_____
_____
_____

What Are Your Views on Science and Scientists?

Teacher Activity: How Do You Define Science?

1. Science is . . .

_____

_____

2. Do you see science as a body of knowledge that has to be memorized? Why? Is this how you were exposed to science?

_____

_____

Teacher Activity: Draw a Scientist

Once you have come up with your own definition for science, draw what you think a scientist looks like:

Now consider these questions:

1. What are your thoughts on what scientists look like?
2. What does your drawing reflect?
3. Why do you think that this is your image of a scientist?
4. How many scientists do you know?
5. Do you have friends who are scientists?
6. Have you always avoided having scientists as friends?

During a recent professional development program, I asked teachers to submit anonymous drawings of scientists. Figure 1.1 shows some randomly selected drawings.

These drawings are rarely representative of scientists, although they do tend to perceive the world slightly differently from nonscientists. Scientists tend to try to find responses to the types of questions that young students are always asking. Scientists are observant, curious, analytical, critical, and objective in their conclusions. In their work, they do not jump to conclusions without first verifying their facts. They constantly use the science process skills.

Figure 1.1 **Teacher Drawings of Scientists**

They are patient, knowing that often it takes a long time to find answers. These drawings represent a naïve view of a scientist; not all scientists work in laboratories or wear lab coats.

What Were Your Early Experiences with Science?

Teacher Activity: Early Experiences with Scientists

As you rekindle some of your earlier childhood curiosity, try to recall some of your earlier experiences with science.

1. As a student, what were your experiences with science?

   _____

   _____

2. What was your experience with the natural world?

   _____

   _____

Teacher Activity: Write Your Science Autobiography

Think back as far as you can. Use these questions to write your science autobiography.

1. What do you recall about your first exposure to science?

   _____

   _____

2. Can you recall events from your elementary classrooms?

   _____

   _____

3. What are your earliest memories of science and your involvement in science?

   _____

   _____

4. Are they good memories?

   _____

As you share your science autobiographies with other teachers, you will see that we have all had varying experiences with science. We have learned from these experiences and want to create opportunities for memorable experiences with science for our budding scientists. What do these activities tell you about your views of science and scientists? Janice Koch (2005) aptly coined the expression "we teach who we are" in discussing science autobiographies. If we have negative stereotypes and perceptions of science and scientists, then that is what we will teach our students. It is extremely important for you to closely examine your view toward science, scientists, and teaching science, because your perceptions and viewpoint will influence how you engage your students in science. Your feelings also impact your expectations and perceptions of students' ability and capacity to do science and become scientists. It is helpful to consider the following points in your approach to teaching science:

- Will your teaching reflect science as a static body of knowledge consisting of one right answer that has to be memorized, or as a constantly expanding dynamic search for answers to questions that arise from our interaction with the natural world and our quest to better understand the world in which we live?

- Will you provide the kinds of experiences that will enable the scientist in each child to emerge?

- Will you enable your students to develop the dispositions that will allow them to continue on their journey to becoming scientifically literate?

Teacher Activity: Write Your Science Story

Think about your experience with science as a young child and write your personal "science story," using these questions:

1. What did you like?

_____

_____

2. What did you hate?

_____

_____

3. How much of it can you remember?

_____

You want your students to have good memories of their science class. You want them to be able to recall some of the questions they had and the process they used for finding answers to those questions.

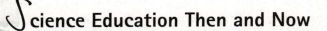

Science Education Then and Now

Science education has changed dramatically since the launching of Sputnik by the Soviet Union in 1957. This is the situation today, as we teach science to young students:

- Student questions guide science activities.
- Students experience examples of concepts before their names are presented.
- Life, physical, and earth sciences are treated in a more balanced way.
- Reading, doing, and thinking about science are combined.
- Mathematics, social studies, and language arts are incorporated into science in a more comprehensive, multidisciplinary way.
- The process skills of science are used to design more meaningful conditions for learning.
- Science learning is recognized as an internalized long-term change in behavior.

To some of us, this is a completely new way of looking at science. It is not the way we were taught, so we need to undergo a paradigm shift in the way we view science teaching and learning.

Many of us find science a difficult subject because we fear the unknown. This hesitancy might also stem from a resistance to change in general. The more uncomfortable you are about doing something, the easier it is to procrastinate or avoid the task entirely. In addition, there may be personal phobias or biases to overcome, including fear of the vast amount of scientific knowledge that is now available. There is no denying that we are living in the midst of an explosion of knowledge that no other generation has ever experienced. We are now surrounded by nanotechnology, plastics, synthetics, numerous electronics devices, computers, video games, lasers, and audio devices. It should come as no surprise that this explosion of knowledge, with its effects on technology, elicits fear in some and insecurity in others—and not just elementary teachers. But if you are willing, you can replace your feelings of fear and insecurity with new skills and knowledge. Additionally, teaching hands-on inquiry science requires far more preparation of physical materials than teaching other subjects. However, the time spent in the preparation is well worth the interest and achievement that you can foster in your students.

Teacher Activity: Final Self-Reflection

Finally, examine this question: How does knowing who you are and who your students are make you a more effective teacher?

_____

_____

_____

_____

_____

_____

_____

Take-Away Thought

Before you can be an effective teacher,
you must know who you are.

How Young Students Learn and Think about Science

2

Focus Questions

- Can you recall your childhood understanding of science?
- What are your students' views of science and scientists?
- What does research say about how students view science and scientists?
- What is science?
- How do students develop an understanding of science?

Can You Recall Your Childhood Understanding of Science?

Spend a few minutes going back in time to when you were a young child. Can you recall how the world appeared to you when you were in elementary school? Did you do science in school? Do you recall doing science outside of school? What did you think science involved? Can you remember what questions you had? Did you ever find answers to those questions?

Teacher Activity: Your Early Recollections of Science

List three things that you can recall about science when you were a young child:

1. _____

   _____

2. _____

   _____

3. _____

   _____

Now consider these questions:

1. Did you recall being very interested in science?

   _____

2. Did you recall any exciting experiences with science?

   _____

3. Did you have happy memories of your interaction with science at that age?

   _____

4. What were your ideas about science then?

   _____

   _____

Some research studies are showing that, starting at grade 3, many students turn away from science, and their interest and participation begin to decline.

Teacher Reflection: Losing Interest in Science

1. Do you recall this happening to you?

_____

_____

2. Do you see it happening to students in your classroom?

_____

_____

3. Are your students excited when it is time for science?

_____

_____

4. Is there time for science? Should science be taught at this level?

_____

_____

Reflect on these questions and discuss with your colleagues. Many of you might not recall any experience with science; we sometimes may block unpleasant memories. Others might recall drawing trees, going on fieldtrips, dissecting flowers, or having scientists visit our classrooms. Whatever your memories, you now want your students to be able to recall later in life pleasant and memorable encounters with science. You want them to recall the experiences they had with you as the "flame" that ignited their interest in science.

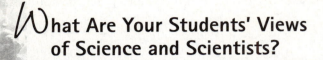

What Are Your Students' Views of Science and Scientists?

Students' views of science and scientists are influenced by the science they do in school, what they experience on field trips and the scientists with whom they interact. Young students need all these interactions to become budding scientists.

Before you begin teaching science, ask your students "What is science?" Their responses might surprise you. Here are some responses from an interview with young students:

- Science is working with trees and plants.
- Science is going to the zoo with my mom.

Third grader in a classroom doing science

Fourth graders on a field trip

Fifth-grade students meeting with a scientist

- Science is looking at a caterpillar turn into a butterfly.
- Science is making a volcano for the science fair.
- Science is growing plants.
- Science is going into space.

As I reflected on these responses, I began to realize that their responses were informed by recent activities conducted during recent science classes, from listening to their siblings talk about science, from watching television.

Classroom Activity: What Is Science?

What responses does your class have for this question?

_____

_____

_____

_____

_____

_____

_____

_____

_____

Once they have given you their definition of science, ask them to draw a scientist.

Classroom Activity: Children's Drawings of a Scientist

Give each student a sheet of paper and ask them to draw a scientist, providing as much detail as possible. Then consider these questions:

1. How do they picture a scientist?

_____

2. Do their drawings reflect the stereotypical view of a scientist (bald or wild hair, male, glasses, pocket protector, lab coat, etc.)?

_____

3. Are their drawings similar to your drawings in Chapter 1?

_____

What Does Research Say about How Students View Science and Scientists?

Barman and his colleagues (2000) investigated children's views of science and scientists. The results of their study indicated that most of the scientists that were depicted in the drawings by students were white males. Students in grades K–2 represented females in drawings more often (42 percent) than students in grades 3–5 (27 percent) and grades 6–8 (25 percent). When depicting the ethnic background of a scientist, 69 percent of grades K–2 students, 80 percent of grades 3–5 students and 74 percent of grades 6–8 students depicted the scientist as Caucasian. This study was conducted in 1999. Since then, there have been major attempts to develop scientific literacy in all our students.

Teacher Activity: Reflection

Consider these questions:

1. Do the drawings and definitions from your students mirror the research findings from the Barman study?

_____

_____

2. Do the definitions and drawings of your students mirror what you have been doing with them in your class?

_____

_____

3. Do you see a difference between the responses of students in the Barman study and your students?

_____

_____

4. What can you do to help your students develop a better understanding of science and scientists?

_____

_____

Remember that you are a significant role model for your students, and they often reflect what you say and do, without your realizing it. If you subconsciously show them that you do not like science or think that scientists are weird, this is what they learn and what gets reflected in their drawings. As you begin to develop your teaching activities, think of strategies you can use to direct your young students away from the negative attitudes toward science and scientists demonstrated by the students in the Barman study.

When you decided to become a teacher, you might not have thought of yourself as a science teacher. It is my hope that in reading here about teaching science to your young students, you will see this as a journey of discovery of strategies that you can use to help students on their pathway to true scientific literacy. As teachers, you need to understand science, the nature of science, and how young students learn science. You also need to develop appropriate instructional skills to help students become scientifically literate.

My work with many elementary teachers has taught me that before you can be confident in your ability to teach science, you need to develop

- a better understanding of science and scientists
- a better understanding of how young students learn science
- appropriate science teaching strategies, resources, and materials
- a way to overcome fear or uncertainty about teaching science

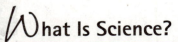

What Is Science?

In a study of over 4,000 teachers, parents, students, and scientists, subjects wrote their definition of the word *science* (Fraser-Abder, 2005). It was a daunting task to filter out of their responses a single and common definition of science. Here are some of those definitions:

Science is . . .

- the constant search for answers about the universe around us
- the study of life and nature
- divided into many different areas—biology, chemistry, physics, etc
- gathering data and then analyzing it
- the study of the world and how it all fits together
- experimentation
- the process of inquiry; the curiosity to explore, to solve problems, and to verify information

As you can see from the examples, there was a wide variation in responses across all respondents. However, as the responses were examined more closely, what emerged was one point of agreement—namely, the dual nature of science as content and process. *Science is an ongoing activity of exploration and the knowledge that comes out of that exploration.* That body of knowledge includes matter, energy, the organisms that inhabit the universe, and the interactions among these organisms and their environment. The exploration that involves observations, measurements, classification, hypotheses, predictions, and, finally, experimentation to verify discoveries and new findings becomes the basis for additional predictions and further explorations. (See Figure 2.1.) This unending journey where each answer leads to more questions represents the process of science. *Scientists are involved in this constant exploration and search for the knowledge that comes from this exploration.* Each new exploration brings new questions, and this is what makes science so interesting and engaging. Scientists are constantly asking What? When? Where? How? and, especially, Why?

Figure 2.1   **Science as the Study of the Interaction among Organisms and Their Environment**

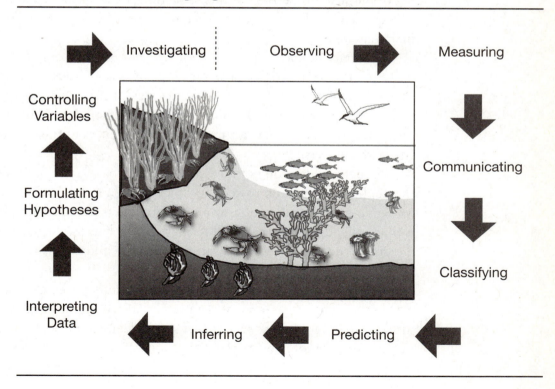

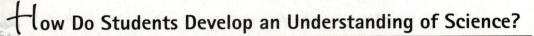

How Do Students Develop an Understanding of Science?

Now that we have a better understanding of science and what scientists do, and know that it is important to teach science, let us take a quick look at how students begin to develop an understanding of physical, life, and earth sciences, as well as some misunderstandings that occur as they learn science. As teachers, we need to learn from the research on child development to further our understanding of how students develop ideas in science. In the following pages, you will find a brief summary of a small part of the research presented in the 2006 report *Taking Science to School* (Duschl et al., 2006). In the list of references for Chapter 2, you will find numerous references to research on students' understanding of science. You will find these books or articles useful reading as you further explore this topic.

Students' Understandings of Physical Properties

Before entering elementary school, students are constantly refining their ideas about objects and the behaviors of those objects over intervals of time and space. By twelve months, children already have a rudimentary understanding of physical properties. At this same time, children are capable of making inferences as to the reasonable and unreasonable causes of the motion of inanimate objects.

Children also have a general knowledge of physical objects but an inability to use this knowledge in a wider range of tasks requiring planning or sequencing of actions. Children learn, however, through a process of trial and error. For example, a child, unlike most adults, would put an object on an unbalanced surface and learn from the consequences of the action the properties of the objects.

Though children do not have a vocabulary base or an understanding of the application of certain scientific concepts such as trajectory, their actions reflect an understanding of how an object moves through space. For example, a child will adjust the angle and strength of the ball they are throwing to anticipate the trajectory. The concepts of force children use to explain the force in physical situations is intuitive.

Concepts in chemistry are foreign to most students before they enter elementary school. Children at the preschool level can distinguish differences in size. However, their conception of size is defined in terms of bigness without an understanding of spatial dimensions. Weight and density have yet to be differentiated as distinct properties of matter. Student's understandings of properties of matter undergo dramatic changes as they begin to understand measures of weight, volume, density, and material type.

Young students are also just beginning to develop concepts of matter that include both solids and liquids. Their understanding is initially grounded in commonsense perceptual properties—such as matter being something you can touch, feel, or see rather than something that has mass and takes up space. The misconception of matter translates into difficulties understanding that matter continues to exist when divided into tiny pieces unable to be seen with the naked eye.

Students' Understandings of Animals

Young students initially have no sense of the living and nonliving world and only think of living things as social beings. It is thought that students' misconceptions with living and nonliving things emerge because animals are understood as social agents with desires, goals, and other thinking and emotional states that explain their actions, whereas plants seem to lack these qualities. Based on psychological similarities to humans, children have a tendency to underattribute biological properties to simpler organisms in the plant and animal kingdom.

Young students are not aware of the mechanisms that underlie biological processes, such as digestion, movement, respiration, and reproduction. On one level, children understand that organisms will physically deteriorate without food and that there is a transformation of food into essential components for use in the body. However, they do not understand that organic molecules release energy units that are used for the contraction of muscles and, subsequently, movement.

During middle school and elementary school, students show major growth in their understanding of the living world as they gain more facts and have more exposure to plants and animals through observations. Children become more aware of what plants and animals do, what their parts are and how those parts work, and what their insides look like—thus gaining a better understanding of structure and function. Though children do become more aware of the structure and function of plants and animals during middle and elementary school, there are still many misconceptions at the cellular level of functioning and mechanics.

Children are quick to learn new concepts and to fit those concepts within the existing conceptual framework. Children will learn that there can be different types of dogs, for instance, or that there are subtypes or new parts or properties of particular kinds of things. But because children already know that animals (such as dogs) can vary in size, body type, and eating preferences, they readily fit new information into the framework of their present knowledge. Subsequently, identifying new kinds of animals that have different clusters of attributes to the ones that children are already familiar with does not fundamentally change their understanding of the organism. Additionally, adding a new superordinate that unites subtypes of animals is not difficult when they are united by common properties that are easy to understand (i.e., learning that bears, dogs, and cats are all mammals).

Students' Understandings of Plants

One of the common misconceptions about plants is that plants are biological mechanisms emerging from the soil. Children do not understand the contribution of carbon dioxide in the developmental process.

As children learn that plants, like animals, are living things, misconceptions often result. Children have a tendency to think that plants behave just like animals and perform activities such as eating and sleeping. Children's misconceptions about the way plants eat are suggestive of the idea that their food is animate and comes from the soil, rather than being synthesized during the process of photosynthesis from sugars in their leaves. Misconceptions about photosynthesis are attributed to students' difficulties understanding matter. This limitation extends to a misconceived understanding of growth and decay.

Students' Understandings of Earth Science

Children's understanding of the world translates into two basic facts: the world is flat, and objects that are unsupported fall down. As children learn more about cosmology and the Earth, they reinterpret their beliefs.

Research has shown that learning about Earth's spherical shape and gravity is a difficult concept for young students. It is not until fourth grade that students are able to better understand both the shape of the Earth as a sphere as well as the concept of gravity working as a force to pull objects towards the center of the Earth. In order for students to better understand the Earth and its forces, it means having a clarification of ideas, thinking through and understanding models, and applying their understandings and conceptual models to observable phenomena.

What Are Some Common Science Misconceptions in Your Classroom?

Teacher Activity: Misconceptions in Your Classroom

1. Can you remember some of your original misconceptions about life, physical, and earth science?

_____

_____

_____

_____

_____

_____

_____

2. Reflect on some science activities you have done with your students. What misconceptions did you note while doing these activities?

_____

_____

_____

_____

_____

_____

_____

The following misconceptions and teaching ideas were recently shared by Laura Henriques (2000) at a science teachers meeting. Table 2.1 was adapted from her presentation.

Table 2.1 Children's Misconceptions and Teaching Ideas

Topic of Misconception	What Students Think	Ideas for Teaching
Worms	Worms help plants grow by getting rid of things that are bad for plants.	Study real worms in your classroom. By studying worms, students will not only learn about worms' role as decomposers, but will also study other important science standards involving animal characteristics and habitats.
Bees	Bees do specific things for the purpose of helping plants.	Organisms carry on activities for the purpose of their own health and survival and, in the process, also become important to other organisms. Do a role-playing pollination simulation with students with a focus on why the bee visits plants and what it does with the nectar it collects.
Soil	Soil provides a support structure and food for plants.	Provide examples of plants that grow in water without soil (e.g., aquariums). Have students germinate seeds in a moist environment without soil, in a nutrient-rich moist environment, without soil, and in moist soil. They will see that the plant germinates and begins to grow in each case, but does not grow as well without nutrients. They will also see that the stem grows upward and the roots downward.
Sunlight	Sunlight helps plants grow by keeping them warm.	Have students grow plants in a warm, lighted environment and compare this with plants grown in a warm, dark environment. Students will see that initially when plants germinate, both sets of plants will grow, but those in the dark are not as green. Over time, the plants in the dark die because, without light, they cannot produce their own food.
Trees and grass	Trees and grass are not plants.	Expose students to various plants by visiting a greenhouse or botanical garden. This will help them understand that there are non-flowering plants and plants that do not always have the typical plant parts that students associate with angiosperms.

As we talk about teaching science to young students, you will see this as a journey of reflections on strategies you can use to help students on their pathway to true scientific literacy. You need to understand science, the nature of science, and how young students learn science if you are to help them become scientifically literate. You also need to develop appropriate instructional skills to help your students become scientifically literate. The activities in this book will support you as you evolve into an outstanding teacher of budding scientists.

Take-Away Thought

Science is an ongoing activity of exploration and the knowledge that comes out of that exploration. Science is process and content.

Your Students and Science Learning

Focus Questions

- Who are your students?
- What are your class' demographics?
- How can you develop a cultural understanding of your students?
- How can you use your students' lived experiences to inform your teaching?
- What are your expectations for your students?
- How can you help grades 3–5 students succeed in science?

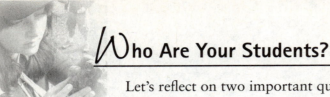

Who Are Your Students?

Let's reflect on two important questions:

- Who are your students?
- What are their lives like?

Regardless of where you teach—urban, suburban, or rural school—you will be faced with an increasingly diverse student population. Table 3.1 shows the dramatically changing demographics in schools in the United States, and Table 3.2 shows the ethnic and geographic distribution. Tables 3.1 and 3.2 have been developed using data from the U.S. Department of Education.

You will note that in two decades the Hispanic and Asian populations have almost doubled. This statistics has implications for the language of instruction and the need for cultural sensitivity. These changing demographics are also reflected in school enrollment in urban, suburban, and rural areas; it is not limited to urban schools. Hence, all teachers have to develop strategies for dealing with an increasingly diverse student population.

Table 3.1 Percentage Distribution (rounded) of Public Elementary and Secondary School Enrollment, by Race/Ethnicity: Selected Years, 1986 to 2005

Year	White, non-Hispanic	Total minority[1]	Black, non-Hispanic	Hispanic	Asian/ Pacific Islander	American Indian/ Alaska Native
1986	70.4	29.6	16.1	9.9	2.8	0.9
1991	67.4	32.6	16.4	11.8	3.4	1.0
1996	64.2	35.8	16.9	14.0	3.8	1.1
2001	60.3	39.7	17.2	17.1	4.2	1.2
2005	57.1	42.9	17.2	19.8	4.6	1.2

[1]Total minority represents persons of all race/ethnicities other than white, non-Hispanic.

Note: Figures do not include students enrolled in Bureau of Indian Affairs (BIA) schools. Detail may not sum to totals because of rounding.

Source: U.S. Department of Education, Office for Civil Rights, *1986 state summaries of elementary and secondary school civil rights survey*; and National Center for Education Statistics, Common Core of Data (CCD), *Public elementary/secondary school universe survey, 1991–92 to 2005–06.*

Table 3.2 — Enrollment in Public Elementary and Secondary Schools, by Race/Ethnicity and Locale: 2005–2006

Locale	Total	White, non–Hispanic	Black, non–Hispanic	Hispanic	Asian or Pacific Islander	American Indian/ Alaskan Native
All public schools	Percentage distribution					
	100.0	100.0	100.0	100.0	100.0	100.0
City	28.5	17.4	46.3	44.3	39.8	18.5
Suburban	36.1	37.2	31.2	35.8	45.9	15.3
Town	13.0	15.9	8.7	9.5	5.1	19.9
Rural	22.4	29.5	13.7	10.4	9.2	46.3

Note: Excludes enrollment for students whose race/ethnicity is unknown.

Source: U.S. Department of Education, National Center for Education Statistics, Common Core of Data (CCD), *Public elementary/secondary school universe survey, 2005–06.*

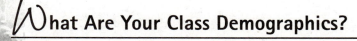

What Are Your Class Demographics?

It might be useful to start the following activity as a private and confidential class profile. Refer to it as you develop your science lesson plans. The information collected here will enable you to respect and cultivate differences among your students.

Teacher Activity: What Are Your Class Demographics?

Class Profile	Traits
	____ Number of students
Gender	____ Girls
	____ Boys

(continued on next page)

Teacher Activity: What Are Your Class Demographics? (continued)

Race	___ American Indian
	___ Asian
	___ Pacific Islander
	___ Filipino
	___ Hispanic
	___ African American
	___ White
	___ Multiple/no response
Religion	___ Christian
	___ Jewish
	___ Muslim
	___ _____
Economic status	___ Wealthy
	___ Comfortable
	___ Struggling
	___ Poor
	___ Homeless
Parents' occupation	___ Parent 1
	___ Parent 2
	___ Caretaker/Guardian
Learning style (based on Gardner)	___ Linguistic
	___ Logical–mathematical
	___ Spatial
	___ Musical
	___ Bodily-kinesthetic
	___ Intrapersonal
	___ Naturalist

(continued on next page)

Teacher Activity: **What Are Your Class Demographics?**
(continued)

Languages   ___ English

                                            ___ Spanish

                                            ___ Vietnamese

                                            _____

Special needs   ___ Fully able

                                            ___ Disability

Technology at home   ___ Computer

                                            ___ iPod

                                            _____

                                            _____

Types of toys at home   _____

                                            _____

                                            _____

                                            _____

Access to   ___ Parks

                                            ___ Gardens

                                            ___ Backyards

Types of pets (if any)   _____

                                            _____

How can you use your knowledge of your class's profile to develop an inclusive
classroom?

_____

_____

_____

_____

_____

The responses to the above question will vary immensely, but here are some ways in which you can use this information to create an inclusive classroom. As an inclusive teacher who is aware of the diversity in your classroom, you must think about your teaching—what you teach, how you teach, and how you structure interactions among your students. All aspects of your classroom life must reflect your commitment to inclusiveness. As part of your curriculum, you should think critically about the kinds of display materials in your room. Do these materials model the belief that we all belong and can all contribute to science? Your books, posters, and other materials should include people of color and of various ethnic backgrounds and people with disabilities. A unit on the five senses should include a discussion on vision and hearing impairments. Consider physical abilities as you plan hands-on activities. Some of your students might not be able to participate in all activities, so you might need to develop alternative experiences for them. Have your students work in mixed-gender groups and have each student occupy different roles. Let them all learn to handle materials and communicate what they are doing to the class.

How Can You Develop a Cultural Understanding of Your Students?

As we begin to develop a contextual framework for teaching science, let us first conduct an in-depth investigation and reflection on the students you teach and your understanding of their lived experiences.

Teacher Activity: Examining Your Classroom's Demographics

Examine your state, district, school, and class data and fill in the following table. You might find that you are unable to fill in all the columns and rows, but do as many as you can.

Demographics	State	District	School	Class
Parental income range				
Free lunch				
English learners				
Compensatory education				
American Indian Asian Pacific Islander Filipino Hispanic African American White Other				
Males Females				

1. What differences do you notice between your state and the national data?

_____

_____

2. What differences do you notice between your class and your state data?

_____

_____

3. Has your district demographics experienced much change in the past four to five years?

_____

_____

4. Is your school experiencing any changing demographics?

_____

_____

Table 3.3 provides an example of these demographics from a district and school on the West Coast.

$\mathcal{T}able$ 3.3 **Example of Demographics of District and School**

Demographics	District A	School 1
Free lunch	4,342	87
English language learners	2,459	44
Compensatory education	2,651	0
Instruction $/student	$3,649	No data available
Instruction—special education $/student	$1,037	No data available
American Indian	25	0
Asian	968	20
Pacific Islander	13	0
Filipino	585	10
Hispanic	6,010	116
African American	464	6
White	7,865	373
Multiple/no response	718	13

As you collect and closely examine this data and the data from your region, you will begin to see trends that will impact what and how you teach. If you are in an urban setting, for example, you might find yourself in a class-room with students who come from twenty to twenty-five different cultures, speak fifteen or more languages, practice twelve or more religions, come from one-parent homes or have two dads or two moms, are homeless, or are extremely wealthy. Those of you who are teaching in the urban setting are already aware of these changing demographics, and you need to be constantly learning about incoming cultures. You might be in a district that shows a beginning change in demographics, with the change not yet reaching your school or your classroom. Be alert. Demographics are changing. You need to begin thinking about how you will accommodate to them. It is critical that you examine this data before you begin to plan for science. The data alerts you to the areas in which you must develop sensitivity and awareness and the expectations you can have of your students and their caregivers. It also helps you determine the types of activities that can be conducted.

Once you have some idea about the bigger picture, you next need to focus in on one diverse student and use this activity to begin to develop your understanding of students who are different. This type of activity is particularly useful if your students belong to a culture that is very different from your own culture.

The place to begin is to collect some background information on what your students' lives are like.

Teacher Activity: Exploring Your Student's Lived Experiences

Visit the home of one student or talk to the student alone. You can also talk to his/her parent(s)/guardian at a school meeting or by telephone about

- expectations for student
- family-perceived views on education, science, future careers, jobs
- discipline
- homework rules
- frequency of family visits to museums, zoos, etc.

Pay special attention to available learning resources, cultural norms, gender roles, and expectations.

Reflect on what you have learned about this student, and develop a plan for integrating what you have discovered in developing teaching and learning strategies for that student.

After interviewing the parents/guardian of one student, you might want to talk to more parents during your parent-teacher meetings or meet parents outside the school setting. Those who live in the community might already have this information. If you do not live or socialize in the community, you can use this activity as a means of beginning to develop your cultural understanding of your students.

Another good starting point in beginning to understand the new cultures moving into your community is the book *Common Bonds* (Byrnes and Kiger, 2005), which examines the growing diversity in schools in a constructive, empowering way.

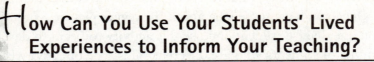

How Can You Use Your Students' Lived Experiences to Inform Your Teaching?

The data you collect in the exercises in this section will inform your philosophical framework for teaching science. This information has implications for your students' access to science and technology materials and field trips and for their knowledge of and interaction with scientists—all important issues you need to consider as you plan for teaching. You might already have been collecting such data for your teaching, but this information is of importance as you plan for science teaching, since it will help you answer important questions such as:

- Can I expect my students' parents/guardian to help them with their science homework?
- Do I need to send letters home in English or in another language?
- What do the parents do for a living? Can I reasonably expect them to provide some resources for me to teach science?
- What parents can I use as facilitators in my class when I expose my students to scientists and what they do?
- Do I have the child/children of a scientist(s) in my class?
- Do parents take their children to zoos, museums, and other nonformal institutions?
- Which parents can I invite to accompany my class on field trips?
- Are there any cultural/religious issues that I should be aware of?

Reflect on these questions and make some quick notes to yourself. What other questions could you add? You can refer back to these notes as you plan your teaching program later on.

How Can You Fit Your Expectations and Experiences to Your Students' Needs?

Teachers need to help both girls and boys develop the self-confidence and skills necessary to be successful. In today's classrooms, girls are rarely told they cannot do both mathematics and science. Textbooks show pictures of women and men in both career and nurturing roles. In preschools, little boys play in the housekeeping center, and little girls play with trucks and blocks. Yet, although doors are opening, the data continue to show that young women have lower self-esteem, lower career aspirations, and lower rates of participation in math and science. Why? Part of the reason is that many women still face internal barriers to success. These are attitudes and fears that result from subtle differences in the ways in which girls and boys are socialized. Even people who are trying to encourage girls may send them negative messages. For example, well-intentioned mathematics teachers may fear discouraging girls, so offer them less criticism than boys, thereby teaching them less. Or they may offer girls premature help, inadvertently suggesting to girls that they probably won't be able to solve the problem alone. Additionally we are moving into an era where many of our boys are dropping out of school. We have to begin to find solutions to these problems from the early grades. As a teacher of young students you play a significant role in encouraging your students to stay in school and to become scientifically literate while enjoying doing science. You can use science as a "hook" to keep them in school. Once you come to a better understanding about who you are as a teacher and what culturally embedded issues your students bring to the classroom, you can begin to focus on the pedagogical issues surrounding teaching budding scientists.

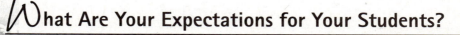

What Are Your Expectations for Your Students?

It is acknowledged in the research community (Grayson and Martin, 2006) that

- People's perceptions about themselves and others shape their expectations for themselves and others in any interactive setting.
- The perceptions and expectations combine to determine how people act in any given situation.
- If a person is in a position of influence with another individual or group of individuals (for example, teacher to student), the influential or more powerful person's perceptions, expectations, and behaviors have a direct impact on the achievement, success, and/or productivity of the individuals with whom he or she has the influence.

Teacher Activity: Teacher Expectations

Spend five to ten minutes quietly reflecting on your expectations for your children. Be as honest as you can be. These are your personal reflections. You do not have to share it with anyone.

1. What are your expectations for your students?

_____
_____
_____

2. Where do you see them fitting into society fifteen to twenty years from now?

_____
_____
_____

3. Will they be manual laborers, engineers, doctors, or teachers?

_____
_____

4. Do you believe they can be scientists?

_____
_____

5. Will they do well in school?

_____
_____

6. Do you believe they can be scientifically literate?

_____
_____

7. What do you think adults need to know about science to be productive members of society?

_____
_____
_____

How Can You Help Grades 3–5 Students Succeed in Science?

The following summarizes what research says you can do to help your students succeed in science:

- Hold high expectations in math and science for all students, especially for minority and female students. Research shows that positive expectations increase student achievement.

- Learn as much about minority and female students as other students in the classroom.

- Respond as fully to the comments of minority and female students as other students.

- Encourage all students. Research shows that minority and female students receive less encouragement.

- Lead a classroom discussion on race and sex stereotyping and its consequence for math and science achievement.

- Involve students who are not participating in classroom discussions. This may include a significant number of minority and female students.

- Do not assume that assertive male students are more capable than female students.

- Make an effort to check classroom work of all students. Some studies report that teachers give more attention to classroom work of male students.

- Encourage all students to participate. Recognize that cultural backgrounds may discourage some students from active participation. In some ethnic groups, volunteering a response or comment is a sign of disrespect of authority.

- Monitor achievement of all students on a daily basis. This includes participation in classroom discussions, experiments, and projects.

- Communicate belief in the potential of minority and female students in math and science. Research indicates many of these students underestimate their potential.

Teacher Activity: Final Self-Reflection

Finally, examine this question: How does knowing who your students are make you a more effective teacher?

_____

_____

_____

_____

_____

_____

_____

_____

_____

Take-Away Thought

Students need to know that you care before they care about what you know.

4

Teaching and Learning Science through Inquiry

Focus Questions

- What is scientific inquiry?

- How important is question-raising in inquiry?

- How can you help your students develop their questioning skills?

- What is guided discovery?

- What is problem-based learning?

- How can process skills be used in inquiry teaching?

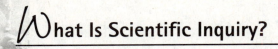

What Is Scientific Inquiry?

The vision of both the *Standards* and the *Benchmarks* is "science and scientific literacy for all." The way in which a child develops scientific literacy depends on experiences both inside and outside the classroom. These experiments will gradually help the child attain more complex modes of thinking. As science instruction in classrooms moves away from the lecture-based, teacher-dominated format, the roles of the teacher and the student change.

In an inquiry-based science learning environment, the teacher's role becomes one of a facilitator—a departure from the role of omniscient presence in the classroom. No longer is the teacher standing in front of the classroom delivering content. Now, the teacher provides the type of environment that guides students to find the answers to the questions they have asked. Once a teacher takes that step of assigning the responsibility of learning to the students, both students and teacher experience a feeling of liberation. It is our job, as teachers, to fill our students with the desire to explore their curiosities and then communicate to us and their peers on what they have learned. Doing that frees the teacher from feeling as though their students' success depends entirely on the teacher, especially when students learn to embrace failure as part of learning. Furthermore, when children take charge of their learning, they often amaze teachers with the approaches that they use, as well as the products of their work. They become the masters of their own learning as they progress through their learning process making predictions, testing hypotheses, revising and ultimately answering questions, and deriving conclusions based on their findings. They are using science content knowledge and science processes together in science inquiry. When young students are engaged in inquiry they

- ask questions
- plan investigations
- collect and interpret data
- share their findings
- overcome misconceptions
- are not limited to understandings set in the lesson goals.

Inquiry is a multifaceted activity that involves

- making observations
- posing questions

- examining books and other sources of information to see what is already known

- planning investigations; using tools to gather, analyze, and interpret data

- reviewing what is already known in light of experimental evidence

- proposing answers, explanations, and predictions

- communicating the results

Inquiry requires identification of assumptions, use of critical and logical thinking, and consideration of alternative explanations (NRC, 1996). Scientific inquiry refers to the diverse ways in which scientists study the natural world and propose explanations based on the evidence derived from their work. Inquiry also refers to the activities of students in which they develop knowledge and understanding of scientific ideas, as well as an understanding of how scientists study the natural world.

Inquiry is central to science learning. When engaging in inquiry, students describe objects and events, ask questions, construct explanations, test those explanations against current scientific knowledge, and communicate their ideas to others. They identify their assumptions, use critical and logical thinking, and consider alternative explanations. In this way, students actively develop their understanding of science by combining scientific knowledge with reasoning and thinking skills.

The importance of inquiry does not imply that all teachers should pursue a single approach to teaching science. Inquiry has many different facets, and teachers need to use many different strategies to develop the understandings and abilities described in the *National Science Education Standards* (NRC, 1996). Furthermore, the *Standards* should not be seen as requiring a specific curriculum. A curriculum is the way content is organized and presented in the classroom. The content embodied in the *Standards* can be organized and presented with many different emphases and perspectives in many different curricula.

What Ideas and Questions Do Your Students Bring to Science?

Children develop their own ideas about the physical world, ideas that reflect their special perspectives.

Students' experiences help them form their ideas, and these often don't match current scientific interpretations. We need to allow our students to ask questions and make mistakes. With time and adequate experiences, they develop scientific understandings.

Many of the reports critical of science education in American schools contain the finding that students are deficient in problem solving or higher-order thinking skills. In addition, science educators who study the kinds of questions asked by teachers and on standardized tests report that most of these questions are lower-level questions that stress memorization and recall thinking by students. If students are to gain skills in using higher-order thinking, they need to be provided with opportunities to use and ask higher-order questions. Teachers first need to develop these skills so that they can then model them in their teaching and develop them in their students.

Teacher Activity: Student Questions on a Nature Walk

Take your class on a nature walk around your school building. List the questions that arise.

_____

_____

_____

_____

_____

_____

_____

Teacher Activity: Student Questions about an Object

Bring a beetle, a growing plant, a robot, or a simple machine into your classroom. Write down the questions that emerge from your students.

_____

_____

_____

_____

_____

_____

As you reflect on these two experiences, do you find that there is a sense of excitement and curiosity in their questions? Did they ask questions about things you have never thought about, things you might not have connected to what they were doing or seeing? This never-ending sense of curiosity, of wanting to know more, is what you have to nurture in your students.

In the following activities, you examine the importance of question raising in developing inquiry-based science. You will

- categorize classroom questions, distinguishing between those that require informational answers and those that are answerable by investigation
- generate action questions from the observation of everyday objects
- establish the relationship between action questions and inquiry

Teacher Activity: Question Raising and Analysis

Imagine that one of your students has found an interesting leaf and has brought it in to show during "Science Share Session." What questions can you ask that will start your students investigating the leaf scientifically? List six to eight questions that will promote investigations.

1. _____

2. _____

3. _____

4. _____

5. _____

6. _____

7. _____

8. _____

Once you have completed your questions, place them in one of the following three columns:

A	??	B

A = questions answerable by information
B = questions answerable by action on the part of the student
?? = questions that may not fit clearly in A or B

Use the information in Table 4.1 to help you analyze your questions.

Table 4.1 Information and Action Questions

A. Information Questions	B. Action Questions
Promote science as information	Promote science as a way of working
Answers derived from secondary sources by talking/reading	Answers derived from first-hand experience involving practical action with materials
Support the trend to emphasize answering as the achievement of a correct end product	Encourage awareness that varied answers may each be "correct" in its own terms and view achievement as what is learned in the process of arriving at an answer
Successful answering is most readily achieved by verbally fluent children who have confidence and facility with words.	Successful answering is achievable by all children and leads to children's feeling of success and confidence.

Teacher Activity: Generating Action Questions

Work with a few colleagues to practice generating action questions. Here are examples of common objects you can use: tennis ball, golf ball, seedling, magnet, bird's nest, bones, seed pods.

In groups of two, select one object and discuss and agree on as many action questions as possible that can be asked about your object.

1. _____
2. _____
3. _____
4. _____
5. _____
6. _____
7. _____
8. _____

Each group should then select their two best action questions for sharing with the larger group.

In this activity, you would have generated action questions you can use in your lesson planning and also as a model for developing students' question-raising skills. As your ability to generate action questions improves, you should keep revisiting and adding questions to the first activity.

Teacher Activity: Developing Broad Questions

In this activity, we will practice changing narrow questions (questions that generate a yes/no or other limited response) to broad questions, which foster a variety of responses. For example:

- *What differences can you find?* This question should draw many possible responses.
- *Can you find differences?* This question may draw only a yes/no response.

Change the following questions to broad questions with multiple possible responses:

1. Are the two objects alike?

   _____

2. Is there anything you notice about this?

   _____

3. Can you think of how this might happen?

   _____

4. Do you remember anything else from the chart?

   _____

5. Are there other ways to do it?

   _____

6. Has it changed?

   _____

7. Can you put these objects in order?

   _____

8. Do you think something else can make a change here?

   _____

Some of your broad questions might look like those in Table 4.2.

Table 4.2 Narrow and Broad Questions

Narrow Questions	Broad Questions
1. Are the two objects alike?	1. In what ways are the two objects alike?
2. Is there anything you notice about this?	2. What do you notice about this?
3. How do you think this might happen?	3. How do you think this might happen?
4. Do you remember anything else from the chart?	4. What else do you remember from this chart?
5. Are there other ways to do it?	5. In what other ways can you do it?
6. Has it changed?	6. In what ways has it changed?
7. Can you put these objects in order?	7. In what ways can you put these objects in order?
8. Do you think something else can make a change here?	8. What else do you think could make a change here?

Teachers engage in two basic kinds of activities as they teach our young students: close ended and open ended. Table 4.3 shows characteristics of close-ended and open-ended questions

Table 4.3 Close- and Open-Ended Questions

Close-Ended Questions	Open-Ended Questions
5 + 5 = ?	? + ? = 12
Single, narrow response	Wide variety of responses
Convergent thinking	Divergent thinking

Once a close-ended activity has made its point; it comes to a close, and the child goes on to something else. When taught well, these activities give students a solid subject matter background that is rooted in experiences, but they tend to be insufficient to promote further inquiry. The outcomes are predictable and specific, and children typically follow someone else's ideas or procedures (teacher or textbook). In open-ended activities, objects and events are described and compared by their observable properties—weight, texture, shape, and so on. This allows students to inspect examples of objects and events that have comparable properties and discover conditions that can change the properties.

Table 4.4 has examples of questions which lead to close-ended or open-ended activities. "I wonder what would happen if. . ." is also a useful way to begin a question for introducing activities.

Table 4.4   Close- and Open-Ended Activities

Close-Ended Activities	Open-Ended Activities
What materials will rust?	In what ways can you get some objects to rust?
How fast does water go up the stems of different plants?	How can you speed up or slow down water rising in different stems?
What things does a nail magnet attract?	How can you make your nail magnet stronger or weaker?
In what kinds of places have you seen mold growing?	What conditions must be present for mold to grow?

Many science programs contain a mixture of close-ended and open-ended activities, often with a larger number of close-ended activities. Although as we discussed earlier, close-ended activities are valuable in learning concepts and procedures, they are limited in improving students' critical thinking skills and ability to function independently. As you develop your plan for teaching, it is helpful if you can spot the close-ended activities that have the potential to be expanded to open-ended activities. Try converting the following typical activity.

Teacher Activity: Sprouting Seeds

Soak a bean seed in water overnight. Plant it in soil. Keep the soil damp. Wait five to six days. What happens to the seed?

1. What broad questions can you ask to open up this activity so students can explore further examples with comparable properties?

_____

_____

2. Despite your broad questions, your students might not think of more objects to try. What narrow questions can you ask that focus on a single object they can try?

_____

_____

(continued on next page)

$\mathcal{T}$eacher $\mathcal{A}$ctivity: Sprouting Seeds (continued)

3. You now want students to explore several conditions that might change or affect the objects in this activity. What broad questions can you ask to do this?

_____

_____

4. You find that your students still lack enough background to ask operational questions about conditions. What narrow questions can you model that include some operations they might try?

_____

_____

Table 4.5 has examples of answers for this Teacher Activity.

In these activities, you have categorized classroom questions, distinguishing between those that require informational answers and those that are

$\mathcal{T}$able 4.5   Examples for Questions

1. What broad questions can you ask to open up this activity so students can explore further examples with comparable properties?	What other seeds will sprout in this way? What, besides a bean seed, do you think will sprout like this? Will sunflower seeds sprout in this way?
2. Despite your broad questions, your students cannot think of more objects to try. What narrow questions can you ask that focus on a single object they can try?	Will radish seeds sprout in this way? How else can you get seeds to sprout beside planting them in damp soil?
3. You now want students to explore several conditions that might change or affect the objects in this activity? What broad questions can you ask to do this?	How can you speed up or slow down the sprouting of seeds? How can you prevent seeds from sprouting?
4. You find that your students still lack enough background to ask operational questions about conditions? What narrow questions can you model that include some operations they might try?	Will bean seeds sprout under water? Will an unsoaked bean planted in damp soil take longer to sprout? Will half of a bean seed sprout?

answerable by investigation, generated action questions from the observation of everyday objects, and begun to establish the relationship between action questions and inquiry.

You have looked at action and information questions and broad and narrow questions and used open- and closed-ended questions to lead to open-ended and close-ended activities.

As you begin to develop your lesson plans, think of ways in which you can make use of these questions to help your students get involved in science. You also need to help your students generate their own questions. This is the beginning of inquiry. Good questions provide the framework for inquiry.

How Can You Develop Inquiry Skills?

Science is a combination of both content and process—learning about the body of knowledge that exists and actively exploring answers to questions you generate about the body of knowledge. You formulate questions that you want to answer through investigation. You also investigate and experience outcomes that make you want to read to understand their meanings. Furthermore, when children involve themselves in discovery and begin to understand what scientists do, they should also begin to realize that they use scientific processes already in normal decision making. We want our young students to learn science by "doing" science, to learn science by generating their own questions and to seek answers to their own questions. It is important for students to have endless "Why" "How" and "What" questions as they interact with their classroom environment and the environment they encounter outside of the classroom. It is also important for them to have many action questions, broad questions, and open-ended questions that lead them to find answers through open-ended activities.

To teach science well means presenting lessons with methods that encourage students to understand the natural world and that actively involve them in discovery that helps them understand what scientists do and find answers to their questions. You want your students to emerge as scientists with endless questions. One way of doing this is to set up a question board in your classroom. Years ago, one of my students described his eight-year-old daughter as a "walking, talking question mark." As teachers, you must guide them in their discovery of answers to these endless questions.

Teacher Activity: The Why Board

Have students write their questions as they are generated. Once or twice per week, set aside a few minutes for "Who has found an answer?" time. Let two or three students tell the class what they now know and what else they want to find out. What new questions do they now have?

Teaching science using inquiry involves having questions generated by students direct their learning experiences. This activity allows your students the time to find answers to the questions they generated.

As your students find answers, let them talk about, draw, or write their responses to share with the rest of the class. You need to keep nurturing this question-asking nature in your budding scientists, and you can frame your curriculum around these questions as much as possible.

Do not supply your students with answers. The emphasis should be on them being scientists and finding answers by investigation, by using the science process skills. One of the most astonishing discoveries a nonscientist can make about science is that there are far more questions than there are answers. It is the asking of questions that makes science so dynamic, and it is the constant searching for the most probable answers that occupies a great deal of scientists' time and efforts. Young students should begin to view science as an interesting question-asking journey. They are discoverers of the unknown. Children are natural investigators. They are always ready to ask questions. Inquiry science comes naturally to them. As teachers your role is to foster the growth of inquiry and to deeply embed in your students the desire to ask questions and to find answers to these questions.

Here are some examples of questions that might appear on your Why Board:

- Will a fan blowing on an ice cube change its melting time?

- Will putting a cube in salt water make it melt slower or faster than it would in fresh water?

- How much longer will a cube of ice last if wrapped in foil or wax paper or newspaper?

- Do people of the same age and weight have the same pulse rate?

- Is your pulse rate different at different times of the day?

These questions represent the beginning of inquiry for your students. Your role is to provide them with the resources to help them find the answers to their questions.

What Are Some Inquiry-Based Teaching Strategies?

Barab and Luehmann (2002), in their research on science teaching, suggest that there is a call for a "new approach" to science education. Central to this call is a shift from a focus on supporting acquisition of formal science content to promoting a culture of scientific literacy by engaging students in the language and ways of scientific inquiry. There should be a shift in the way that science is taught. This shift is from a more traditional lecture-driven science curriculum to a more active, inquiry-based curriculum. The authors propose that the driving force behind the movement to an inquiry curriculum can be attributed to a view of students as global citizens rather than as vessels to be filled with facts. Subsequently, science education should attempt to provide students with a better understanding of the world around them while recognizing that not all of them will be future scientists

In order to approach science in a novel way, moving away from rote memorization of facts for later regurgitation, the literature suggests that it is important to engage students in scientific inquiry. This scientific inquiry should be in the context of authentic and sustained scientific investigations, allowing students to not only learn the content of science but also to master the inquiry/doing process of science as well.

By the time children begin school, they have lived scientifically for at least a few years. They have been curious, identified problems, asked questions, and sought answers. School science, when it is offered, adds a new dimension, with children now being guided in their quest for answers through the provision of carefully selected learning activities, materials, and teaching strategies. In the elementary classroom, where children are continuously generating their own questions, inquiry, guided discovery, and problem-based learning strategies are most applicable.

Guided Discovery

Students begin with questions and materials that will help them find answers to the questions. Your class can be divided up into small groups and given the time to observe, explore, and discover the answers to the questions. As your students explore, you serve as the facilitator or guide to this discovery. As facilitator, you are responsible for

- supplying the initial question/s to initiate exploration
- providing relevant materials/resources
- listening to each group as they explore

- keeping them on track with their exploration
- providing materials that will move the exploration forward

As students explore, you must always keep in mind that they have to come up with their own answers; you are not there to supply the answers. Always redirect questions to them by using such responses as: What do you think? or Can you try out your partner's idea? You allow children the time to explore, to "mess about" with the materials, and in the process to find answers to their interesting questions. As you move around the class, you should give only minimal assistance to ensure that students are not unduly frustrated and quit. You must not tell students what you want them to learn or give answers. You want them to discover the answers on their own, with minimal guidance from you. When using this method, the question could be generated by the students, the text, the lesson plan, or you. You can help students seek text-based answers if they cannot find answers through their own material exploration.

In summary, during guided discovery you will

- engage students in activities

- encourage them to explore concrete materials and reflect on their findings

- engage students in conversations, listen to their ideas, and provide guidance to help them build and test their own explanations of what is happening (Koch, 1999, p. 12).

Problem-Based Learning

Students are presented with a challenge (such as a question to be answered, an observation or data set to be interpreted, or a hypothesis to be tested) and will accomplish the desired learning in the process of responding to that challenge. As with all inductive methods, the information needed to address the challenge would not have been previously covered explicitly in lectures or readings. Students usually working in teams are confronted with an open-ended real-world problem to solve and take the lead in defining the problem precisely and in figuring out what they know, what they need to determine, and how to proceed in determining it. They formulate and evaluate alternative solutions, select the best one and make a case for it, and evaluate the lesson learned. When they identify the need for instruction on new material, you either provide it or guide them to obtain the required information themselves. In problem-based learning, students have not previously received formal instruction in the necessary background material, and the solution process is more important than the final product.

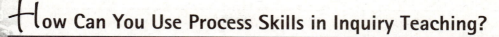

How Can You Use Process Skills in Inquiry Teaching?

To be good inquiry learners, we must develop and use process skills, since these are the building blocks of inquiry.

Every day is filled with opportunities to learn science content and use science process skills. You can begin with introducing your young students to the natural world by encouraging them to observe what goes on around them.

You can guide them to

- see how long it takes for a dandelion or a rose to burst into full bloom
- watch the moon as it appears to change shape over the course of a month and record the changes
- watch a caterpillar change into a butterfly
- bake a cake
- guess why one of your plants is drooping

As you provide observation activities, use activities of varying lengths. This is important for students with attention deficits. As you get their interest, you can gradually give them lengthier activities.

The processes of science are basic components of thinking and are useful in problem solving and critical thinking, not only in science but also in day-to-day life situations. As young students enter school, it is critical to emphasize individual processes to help them become proficient in using the processes. They are then introduced to activities in which the use of processes is combined with domain-specific knowledge, as determined by the *benchmarks*.

As you research the process skills, you will find a variation from state to state or program to program. These skills represent the range of activities in which scientists engage and which students need to become fully scientifically literate and capable critical thinkers. A comprehensive and representative list of process skills is included below.

Teacher Activity: Process Skills

Go to your state Website and print out the process skills that are listed. Then, fill in the table. (See Table 4.6.)

Table 4.6 Process Skills

Process Skill	Definition	Check if listed for your state
Observing	becoming aware of an object or event by using any of the senses to identify properties	
Measuring	making quantitative observations by comparing to a conventional or nonconventional standard	
Classifying	sorting objects, events, or information representing objects or events in classes, according to some method or system	
Communicating	giving oral or written explanations or graphic representations of observations	
Inferring	drawing a conclusion based on prior experiences	
Predicting	making a forecast of future events or conditions expected to exist	
Hypothesizing	constructing a tentative answer to a problem from generalized observations	
Interpreting data	analyzing data that have been obtained and organized by determining apparent patterns or relationships in the data	
Controlling variables	discriminating among factors that will or will not affect the outcome of an experiment	
Experimenting	designing and carrying out procedures to obtain information about interrelationships between objects and events	

How Do You Use Process Skills in Your Daily Life?

In your day-to-day activities, you, too, use these skills. There are many daily instances in which you must act like a scientist.

Teacher Activity: A Damaged Computer

Your laptop computer has been damaged in a flood at your school. How do you go about solving your problem? What do you do? Should you dump it? Can it be saved? List the steps you take and the questions you ask. List the process skills you engage in as you make a decision.

Before you purchase an appliance (such as a washing machine), you spend time investigating the pros and cons of one brand versus another. You are curious about energy consumption, level of noise, load capacity, control panel etc. You analyze the product in terms of your needs. You go on the Internet and check consumer reports. You ask friends who have the brands you are interested in, compare prices, check for sales, and finally make an objective decision based on your tentative conclusions. You then buy the product that best meets your needs. In this investigation, you have used many of the processes that scientists use as they engage in science. This is yet another reason to develop students' scientific skills.

Take-Away Thought

Everyone uses process skills in their daily decision making.

Exploring Process Skills with Your Students

Focus Questions

- How can you develop observation skills?
- How can you develop measuring skills?
- How can you develop communication skills?
- How can you develop classifying skills?
- How can you develop predicting skills?
- How can you develop inference-making skills?

- How can you begin to formulate hypotheses?
- How can you develop skills in interpreting data?
- How can you develop skills in controlling variables?
- How can you develop investigating skills?
- How well do you know the process skills?

Process Circus

It is critical that, as a grades 3–5 teacher, you experience the processes so that you can better incorporate them in your inquiry teaching.

The following activity could best be used by a staff developer to introduce teachers to the science process skills.

Teacher Activity: Process Circus

Purpose: To clarify the meaning of each process skill in practical action terms, and to arrive at a group understanding of the process skills.

Procedure:

- Brief introduction
- Practical work on circus
- Small group discussions to combine results and reflect upon the meaning of each process skill
- Whole group plenary discussion

Preparation: You should create 10–14 brief practical items, each of which has a specific process skill as its main focus. Here are examples of six items with required equipment in italics:

1. Draw and label what you think a candle looks like when it is lit. Light the candle and draw it again. What is different from what you first drew? *Candle and matches.*

2. Measure the amount of water that drips from the tap in one minute. Work out how much water will drip away in one day. *10 or 25 ml measuring cylinder, stop-clock, sink with tap dripping at a steady pace.*

3. If you have three different types of soil, how would you find out which holds the most water?

4. Put ice in the can. Look at the outside of the can. Write down as many possible explanations as you can of what you see. *Clean empty shiny can without lid, ice cubes.*

5. Every twig tells the story of its own life. Closely examine your twig and tell the story of its life. *Twig with buds and scars, but no leaves or flowers, hand lens.*

6. Divide the leaves into as many groups as you can. *10–12 varying colored and shaped fall leaves.*

Write each item on a card and lay them out around the room in any order. Each item should have the required equipment.

Introduction: Participants are asked to work in pairs to carry out the task on each card using only the equipment given. They use the following grid for recording their decisions about the process skills they use in carrying out each task.

(continued on next page)

Teacher Activity: Process Circus (continued)

Process skills/Circus item	1	2	3	4	5	6
Observing						
Measuring						
Communicating						
Classifying						
Predicting						
Inferring						
Interpreting data						
Formulating hypotheses						
Controlling variables						
Investigating						

Each group is to indicate by checking off in the grid for each item the process skills they think they used. There may be more than one process skill and it may be that some are felt to be predominant in an item. They can use their own way of indicating this weighting.

Practical work: Participants go around the "circus" carrying out the activities. They must do what is on the card and not just read and respond without carrying out the task themselves. This ensures that they experience the process and can reflect on what they actually did, not just the verbal description. After each activity, they must also fill in the grid about the process skills used.

Small group discussion: Participants are now formed into groups of 6–8 to discuss each item of the circus and to try to arrive at a group consensus on the process skills used. Where there are differences, they must justify their views. In doing so, differing views about the meaning of the process skills are revealed and the discussion helps individual members refine and revise their own ideas.

Plenary discussion: One group is chosen to present its results item by item. Other groups will report on differences between what is presented and their own views. These differences have to be reconciled by appeal to evidence of the circus items, justification from the group or by reference to the indicators found at the end of each process section in the chapter. At all times the purpose of the exercise should be kept in mind, i.e. the clarification and greater shared understanding of the process skills. At the end of this discussion, participants should arrive at definitions which they have helped to generate for each process skill and should all have a better understanding of each process skill. Participants will note that often, it is not possible to tease out a single process from an activity, since the processes tend to be closely interwoven (e.g., you cannot communicate without first observing or classify without first observing). It is virtually impossible to present each process as a discrete, isolated, totally unique action. Often, you will be using several skills in order to better understand one particular skill. You will soon see that the overlap and interplay among the processes is not only inevitable but also essential in scientific inquiry.

The following activities are designed to involve teachers in developing an understanding of the process skills followed by reflection, analysis and development of process based activities for their own classroom.

How Can You Develop Observation Skills?

Observing is a process through which you become aware of objects and events. Observation involves the use of any one of the senses alone (touch, taste, smell, sight, and hearing) or the senses in combination. Observing is a skill that can always be improved. No one can ever say that they have mastered the skill of observing. Generally, the more opportunities you have for observing, the more you will improve your use of this skill. The following activity can strengthen both your skill of observing and your awareness of your environment.

Teacher Activity: A-Ten Minute Observation Walk

Take a ten-minute walk around your school.

What do you see? (trees, cracks in the school wall. etc.)

_____

_____

What do you hear? (water dripping, loud music, birds, crickets, etc.)

_____

_____

What do you smell? (car exhaust, leaves, etc.)

_____

_____

Is there anything in the environment that you can taste? (clover, water, etc.)

_____

_____

What can you touch? (rough surfaced wall, etc.)

_____

_____

Classroom Activity: Writing Observation Activities

Safety note: Because of health concerns, you must not allow young children to taste without permission from parents. Before involving them in an activity involving taste you should send a letter home to parents and get their written consent.

Encourage your students to observe nature, using all of their senses. Based on what we have just done, write two simple observing activities for use with your class.

1. First observation activity

_____

_____

_____

2. Second observation activity

_____

_____

_____

Process Indicator

Students are observing when they can

- identify the properties of objects (such as color, size, and shape) by using any or all of the senses and can answer this type of question: What do you notice about these objects?

- state noticeable changes in objects or event and can answer this type of question: What changes do you notice?

- state noticeable similarities and differences in objects or events and can answer this type of question: How are they alike? Different?

How Can You Develop Measuring Skills?

By measuring, we are able to increase the precision of our observations and provide a means of recording our observations. We must decide what measurements should be taken and what instruments should be used. Should we use a measuring cylinder, a ruler, or a balance? What units should we use?

Teacher Activity: Measurement

This activity will involve you in the process of measuring. You will make linear measurements, liquid measurements, and mass/weight measurements.

1. Linear measurement

   Select a nonstandard measuring device, identify it by some means, and measure the same object or distance in the room, using the selected device. Body parts such as hands, feet, or arms make good nonstandard measuring devices.

   Record your data.

   - Identify your measuring device.

   - Identify what was measured.

   - Identify the distance measured.

   - Is the recorded measurement consistent with the type of measuring device used? For example, if you selected a paper clip as the measuring device, the object or distance measured should be recorded as so many paper clips in length.

   - If you are working with a partner, did you use the same device for measuring? For example, if you both chose to use a hand as the measuring device, then the same hand must be used for all measurements. Hands come in different sizes, as do other devices that might be used in measuring distances. It is very important that a standard be established so that measurement can be related.

2. Liquid measurement

   Select two containers; one should be much larger than the other. Identify each by some means and use the smaller container to determine the amount of liquid that the larger container holds.

   Record your data.

   - Identify your measuring device.

   - Identify what was measured.

   - Identify the amount measured.

   - Is the recorded measurement consistent with the type of measuring device used? For example, if you identified the measuring device as "a small cup," then the amount recorded should be in so many small cups.

   - Did you establish a way to handle the problem of describing the amount measured when the measuring device was only partially filled? If not, do so now.

(continued on next page)

Teacher Activity: Measurement (continued)

3. Mass/weight measurements

   Select an object and measure its mass/weight using an equal-arm balance. Place the object to be measured on one side of the balance and measure its mass/weight by placing paper clips on the other side until it balances. Record your data.

   - Identify the object to be measured.

   - What was the mass/weight of the object?

   - Is the mass/weight of the object recorded so that it is clear that paper clips were the standard?

   - What other things could you use as a standard for measuring mass/weight?

   When you have completed the three parts of this activity, answer the following:

   - How were you involved in the process of measuring?

   _____

   _____

   _____

   _____

   _____

   - Can you explain this process?

   _____

   _____

   _____

   _____

   _____

   - How important is it to identify a standard when making measurements?

   _____

   _____

   _____

   _____

   _____

Classroom Activity: Write Measuring Activities

Now that you have had some experience with measuring, how can you transfer these ideas to your classroom? Write three measuring activities that you can use.

1. Activity 1

_____

_____

2. Activity 2

_____

_____

3. Activity 3

_____

_____

Process Indicator

Students are measuring when they can

- arrange objects in sequence by length (shortest to longest), weight (lightest to heaviest), volume (least to greatest), chronologically (beginning to end), numerically (in ordinal order)

- use standard tools—such as the meter stick, yardstick, ruler, clock, balance, and protractor—to find quantity

How Can You Develop Communicating Skills?

Communication is conveying information by means of oral or written descriptions, pictures, graphs, maps, or demonstrations. Communicating in science refers to the skill of describing simple phenomena. A written or oral description of physical objects and systems and of the changes in them is one of the most common ways of communicating in science. Communicating takes many forms—identifying, matching, sorting, naming, comparing, contrasting, grouping, distinguishing likenesses and differences, relating observations, and using words accurately. Drawings, data charts, graphs, and journals are all used in recording and communicating descriptions of science experiences and results of experimentation.

Teacher Activity: Communicating with a Friend

This activity will involve you in the process of communicating. You need to work with a partner to complete this activity. Take a walk with your partner. As you walk, begin to describe an object that you have selected. You must describe the object so clearly and accurately that your partner must be able to identify it on the first try.

Communicating serves two purposes:

- to ensure that knowledge of concepts and relationships is accurately recorded
- to share findings with others

Classroom Activity: Communicating

Now that you have had some experience with communicating, how can you transfer these ideas to your classroom? Write two communicating activities for use with your class.

1. Activity 1

_____

_____

2. Activity 2

_____

_____

Process Indicator

Students are communicating when they

- describe objects or events, and can answer this type of question: How can you describe this _____ so someone else knows what you mean?
- make charts and graphs, and can answer this type of question: How can you make a chart or graph to show your findings?
- record data as needed, and can answer this type of question: How can we keep track of our observations?
- construct exhibits and models, and can answer this type of question: How can we show someone how this works?

- draw diagrams, pictures, and maps, and can answer these types of questions: What can we draw to explain what happens? What map can you draw so someone else can find the place?

How Can You Develop Classifying Skills?

As students engage in classifying, they are identifying, matching, sorting, naming, comparing, contrasting, grouping, and distinguishing likenesses and differences.

One of the ways in which knowledge obtained from scientific inquiry can be organized is through classification. For example, plants and animals are two of the five major kingdoms into which living things in the world can be grouped. Within each there are subclasses, and within these, there are more subclasses. This system provides a way to organize a vast amount of information.

Teacher Activity: Classifying Animals

Classify the animals in the picture based on criteria you have selected.

1. Identify and label each group according to the property you used to separate the groups.

   a. Organize the pictures into two groups. Record the property used to make the separation.

   b. Find another way to separate the pictures into two groups. Label the two new groups.

   c. Take about three minutes and see how many different ways you can divide the pictures into two groups. Label each group.

2. Now that you have had some practice in grouping, or classifying, objects into two sets, try to separate the pictures into three groups. Make as many sets of three as you can and label them.

3. Check over your list to see that all the pictures fit into one of the groups in each set. But make sure that no one picture could fit into both groups of one set.

Teacher Activity: Questions to Develop Classifying Skills

If you were trying to help students develop the skill of classifying, what questions might you ask to encourage them to investigate the various properties that could be used in grouping the objects?

List some questions:

_____

_____

_____

_____

_____

_____

_____

Process Indicator

Students are classifying when they

- group objects or events by their properties or functions, and can answer questions such as: In what ways could we group these objects?

- arrange objects or events in order by some properties or value, and can answer questions such as: How could we put these objects in order?

How Can You Develop Predicting Skills?

Predicting is the ability to state a future occurrence based on a pattern formed from previous observations. A prediction can only be made after a series of observations and measurements have been made and their relationships determined. On the basis of the analysis of collected data, you can predict or forecast what will happen next. In order to make a reasonable prediction, you must be clear about the difference between a guess and a prediction. A guess is a statement based on no data or very little data. A prediction is a statement based on a lot of data. You should write down your data and then look for a pattern. You may need to prepare a graph, and extend the graph, following the pattern it seems to follow.

By developing skills of thinking systematically and logically about what might happen next, you can begin to think about planning ahead. Making a prediction is very different from just guessing; predictions should be based on selected data. Two types of predictions are possible using graphically presented data: (1) interpolation, within the data, and (2) extrapolation, beyond the data. In both types of predictions, data are gathered and recorded in graph form. A pattern should emerge and the prediction is made. The following activity is designed to help you engage in the process of predicting.

Teacher Activity: Predicting Dissolving Time

If two sugar cubes take a certain time to dissolve in water at room temperature, and dissolve faster and faster as you increase the temperature from 10°C to 20°C to 40°C, you may form a pattern with respect to the time the cubes take to dissolve as the temperature increases. So, you may be able to predict how long sugar cubes will take to dissolve at a temperature of 60°C. You may draw a graph to help in your prediction.

Plan two activities for your class involving the use of predicting.

1. Activity 1

   _____

   _____

   _____

   _____

2. Activity 2

   _____

   _____

   _____

   _____

   _____

Process Indicator
Students are predicting when they

- think systematically and logically about what might happen next
- begin to think about planning ahead

How Can You Develop Inference-Making Skills?

It is important that you learn to distinguish between observations and inferences. An observation is made through one or more of the senses. An inference is an explanation of an observation or a number of observations. The inference you make may be reasonable, but it may or may not be correct. An inference could be described as an educated guess. It is an interpretation or an explanation based on observations. It is a speculation from immediate observation.

Teacher Activity: Making Inferences

Example: You were sleeping for the last hour. You get up and you go outside. The ground is wet, the car is wet. You can see and feel that the ground and the car are wet; these are observations. You did not see the rain falling, so if you say that rain fell, you are making an inference. Your inference may or may not be correct. Someone could have sprayed the ground and the car with a garden hose. However, your inference is a reasonable one.

List examples of two inferences:

1. _____

   _____

   _____

2. _____

   _____

   _____

Process Indicator
Students are inferring when they

- understand that their explanations of an observation may be reasonable but may or may not be correct

One of the greatest benefits of being able to distinguish between an observation and an inference is a decrease in the tendency to jump to conclusions. Observations help us become more aware of our world, and adequate use of inferences makes us more curious as well as more cautious in jumping to conclusions. Inferences should always be tentative, limited, subjective, and informed by previous experiences.

How Do You Begin to Formulate Hypotheses?

Formulating hypotheses suggesting reasons for events or phenomena that can be tested scientifically involves applying concepts and ideas from previous experiences.

Process Indicator

Formulating includes

- attempting to explain observations or relationships in terms of some principle or concept
- applying concepts or knowledge gained in one situation to help understand or solve a problem in another
- recognizing that there can be more than one possible explanation of an event
- realizing the need to test explanations by gathering more evidence

Students are hypothesizing when they

- can identify relevant previous experiences that suggest explanations of new phenomena and can entertain alternative possible explanations

Teacher Activity: Formulating Hypotheses

Given five different brands of paper towels, formulate a hypothesis to answer the following question: Does the brand of paper towel affect the amount of water it will hold?

Formulate and then test your hypothesis. Then compare your hypothesis to the actual results you obtain and tell whether or not your hypothesis was correct.

_____

_____

_____

_____

_____

Classroom Activity: Activities for Formulating Hypotheses

Now that you have had some experience with formulating hypotheses, how can you transfer these ideas to your classroom? Write two activities in which your students will formulate and then test their hypothesis.

1. _____
   _____
   _____
   _____
   _____
   _____

2. _____
   _____
   _____
   _____
   _____
   _____

How Do You Develop Skills in Interpreting Data?

Interpreting data includes putting several pieces of information together and making some sense of the whole.

Process Indicator

Interpreting data also involves

- identifying trends or correspondences or relationships
- drawing conclusions
- putting various pieces of information (from direct observations or secondary sources) together and inferring something from them
- using patterns or relationships in information, measurements, or observations to make predictions
- realizing the difference between a conclusion that fits all the evidence and an inference that goes beyond it
- being able to check possible relationships carefully with evidence and recognize trends in data even when patterns are not exact

Teacher Activity: Interpreting Data

Four boys (Gerald, Ian, Michael, and Stephan) played with their friends over the midterm holiday. Below is a list of whom they each played with:

- Gerald: Frank, Nicolas, Gabriel, John, Ralph, Paul
- Ian: Frank, Anthony, Gabriel, John, James, Paul
- Michael: Frank, Gabriel, John, Ralph, Jason, Edward
- Stephan: Frank, Anthony, Gabriel, Eric, Peter, James

When it was time to return to school, Gerald, Ian, and Michael all had the flu. The doctor said they must have caught it from one of the friends they played with over the holiday.

1. Which friend do you think they could have caught the flu from?

_____

2. How did you decide?

_____

_____

_____

Classroom Activity: Data Interpretation Activities

Now that you have had some experience with interpreting data, how can you transfer these ideas to your classroom? Write two activities in which your students will interpret some data that you present to them.

1. _____

_____

_____

2. _____

_____

_____

_____

Ηow Do You Develop Skills in Controlling Variables?

Process Indicator

Controlling variables includes

- proposing how to find out something through practical manipulation of materials
- recognizing the variables to be controlled and those to be changed, and how this is to be done
- deciding how to collect and record relevant data
- identifying what is to change or be changed when different observations or measurements are made

Τeacher Αctivity: Controlling Variables

In an investigation to determine whether a certain brand of paper towel will absorb salt water faster than tap water, the following variables may affect the outcome of the investigation:

1. the size of the paper

2. the type of water

3. the amount of water absorbed

4. the rate at which the water is absorbed

5. the amount of water used

Two variables that must be held constant (must not be changed) are

A. 1 and 5 only   C. 3 and 4 only

B. 2, 4, and 5 only   D. 1, 2, and 3 only

[ANSWER: A]

Now that you have had some experience with controlling variables, how can you transfer these ideas to your classroom? Write two activities in which your students will demonstrate their ability to control variables.

1. _____

_____

2. _____

_____

How Do You Develop Investigating Skills?

Process Indicator
Investigating includes

- investigating using materials and scientific concepts to create procedures for solving practical problems
- deciding what equipment and material are needed for an investigation
- identifying what is to be changed when different observations or measurements are made
- identifying what variables are to be kept the same for a fair test
- identifying what is to be measured or compared
- considering beforehand how measurements and comparisons are to be used to solve the problem
- deciding the order in which steps should be taken in the investigation

Teacher Activity: Investigating Skills

Given a tennis ball and a golf ball, design an investigation to determine which ball bounces the highest.

1. Describe what you will do to determine which ball bounces the highest.

2. Do the investigation.

3. Construct a chart to show your results.

4. Graph the results.

5. What did you learn from this investigation?

_____

_____

_____

_____

_____

_____

Classroom Activity: Investigating Skills Activities

Now that you have had some experience with investigating, how can you transfer these ideas to your classroom? Write two activities in which your students will plan and complete an investigation.

1. Activity 1

_____
_____
_____
_____
_____
_____
_____
_____

2. Activity 2

_____
_____
_____
_____
_____
_____
_____
_____
_____
_____

How Well Do You Know Process Skills?

You can ask questions to start students thinking about any of the process skills, as in the following activity.

Classroom Activity: Matching Skills

Below is a list of process skills and questions. Each question goes with one of the skills. Match each question with the proper skill involved.

Process Skills

A. Observing

B. Classifying

C. Measuring

D. Communicating

E. Predicting

F. Formulating hypotheses

G. Interpreting data

H. Controlling variables

I. Investigating

Question Clusters

- What do you think will happen?

- What did you find out? What story do the small footprints tell?

- How could you put these objects together? In what groups do they belong?

- How could these things be put into some order?

- What do you notice?

- How are these objects alike? Different?

- How does this compare to how it was before?

- How heavy (light, fast, slow, tall, etc.) is it?

- What could you use instead of a meter stick?

- How can you estimate how many peas are in jar?

- How can you show your findings on a chart?

- How can you keep a record of your work?

- Which rubber band will stretch the most when 16 ounces are added?

- Which variable did you change?

- What is the difference in height between plant A and plant B?

- The objects that are small and light will fall the fastest.

Answers: E, D, B, B, A, A, A, C, C, C, D, D, I, H, G, F

Research on learning (not only in science but across the curriculum) shows that students learn more, remember more of what they learn, and are more likely to use what they learn if they are asked to take more responsibility for their own learning. Students are more likely to learn science if they explore natural phenomena directly, pose their own questions, design their own experiments, and discuss the results with others. Though poorly designed experiments contribute little to learning, a teacher who understands how to help students set up an appropriate experiment can contribute much to student learning.

Moreover, the evidence shows that not all children profit from the same teaching techniques. Some children learn better through cooperation with others than through either solitary work or competitive activities. There is strong evidence that many students would learn more science and like it better if teaching methods required students to be more active and interactive than they are in most of today's science classes. Learning science, like learning mathematics and a foreign language, is a cumulative process. To fully grasp the meaning of science, students need a steady supply of experiences with the natural world, repeated opportunities to raise questions and answer them, and time to develop skills and attitudes that are needed to understand and to do science.

Take-Away Thought

Your students become budding scientists as they use their senses to observe, measure, classify, communicate, predict, infer, formulate hypotheses, control variables, interpret data, investigate, and experiment.

6

Establishing Your Science Program

Focus Questions

- What are the Big Ideas in science?

- What concepts should you include in your curriculum?

- How do you build an effective science learning environment?

- How can you set up your classroom for science?

Remember, you are not alone in teaching science. There are numerous resources all around you. Many of them you have not thought of, many of them you do not know exist, and many you pass by on a daily basis and do not think of as a science teaching resource. Do you know that you can take your class on a field trip in your school? We will first consider what content we need to know to begin the journey for teaching science to young students. Then, in the following chapter, we will examine the numerous resources that you can use to help you on your journey. In order to assist you in your preparation, you will find in the appendixes:

- the requirements of the *National Science Education Standards,* the *Benchmarks for Science Literacy,* and state standards, which provide the context in which you will be teaching science
- the content knowledge teachers need to feel confident in their ability to teach the required science and to provide a framework for developing quality science learning experiences for grades 3–5 students

What Are the Big Ideas in Science?

Just as science processes are subdivided, science content, too, is organized into key concepts, which are the foremost ideas around which science is organized. Students can learn these key concepts as a consequence of their experiential inquiry. When you have a clear idea of the concepts you wish students to ascertain from an experience, the students will be more apt to learn those concepts. It is important, therefore, that you be as well versed in the subject matter of science as possible. In addition, by knowing the basics of what your students need to know by the end of the fifth grade, you will be more confident in your teaching and feel less fearful of teaching science. As an elementary teacher, if you are open to learning about science and seeing it as a process, as well as knowing how to use the scientific process to be a good facilitator, you can get started on having successful science experiences with your students. This way, you begin to enjoy teaching science and want to learn more about concepts and content.

More than a decade ago the National Center for Improving Science Education recommended that elementary schools design curricula that introduce nine scientific concepts. The nine concepts, the Big Ideas of science, are still relevant to today's elementary student:

Big Ideas in Science

- Organization
- Cause and effect

- Systems
- Scale
- Models
- Change
- Structure and function
- Variation
- Diversity

1. **Organization.** Scientists have made the study of science manageable by organizing and classifying natural phenomena. For example, natural objects can be assembled in hierarchies (atoms, molecules, mineral, grains, rocks, strata, hills, mountains, and planets). Or objects can be arranged according to their complexity (single-celled amoeba, sponges, and so on, to mammals).

2. **Cause and effect.** Nature behaves in predictable ways. Searching for explanations is the major activity of science; effects cannot occur without causes. Young students can learn about cause and effect by observing the effect that light, water, and warmth have on seeds and plants.

3. **Systems.** A system is a whole that is composed of parts arranged in an orderly manner according to some scheme or plan. In science, systems involve matter, energy, and information that move through defined pathways. The amount of matter, energy, and information, and the rate at which they are transferred through the pathways varies over time. Students begin to understand systems by tracking changes among the individual parts and by studying ecosystems to see the interaction between plants and animal life.

4. **Scale.** Scale refers to quantity, both relative and absolute. Thermometers, rulers, and weighing devices help students see that objects and energy vary in quantity. It is hard for students to understand that certain phenomena can exist only within fixed limits of size. Yet young students can begin to understand scale if they are asked, for instance, to imagine a mouse the size of an elephant. Would the mouse still have the same proportions if it were that large? What changes would have to occur in the elephant-sized mouse for it to function?

5. **Models.** We can create or design objects that represent other things. Students can gain experience by drawing a picture of a cell as they observe it through a microscope. They can also use paper to build a plane, or use a variety of arts and crafts materials, along with consumables such as paper clips and cotton balls, to design and build a model house or car.

6. **Change.** The natural world continually changes, although some changes may be too slow to observe. Rates of change vary. Students can be asked to observe changes in the position and apparent shape of the moon. Parents and students can track the position of the moon at the same time each night and draw pictures of the moon's changing shape to learn that

change takes place during the lunar cycle. Students can also observe and describe changes in the properties of water when it boils, melts, evaporates, freezes, or condenses.

7. **Structure and function.** A relationship exists between the way organisms and objects look (feel, smell, sound, and taste) and the things they do. Students can learn that skunks spray a bad odor to protect themselves. Students also can learn to infer what a mammal eats by studying its teeth or what a bird eats by studying the structure of its beak.

8. **Variation.** To understand the concept of organic evolution and the statistical nature of the world, students first need to understand that all organisms and objects have distinctive properties. Some of these properties are so distinctive that no continuum connects them—for example, living and nonliving things, or sugar and salt. In most of the natural world, however, the properties of organisms and objects vary continuously.

9. **Diversity.** This is the most obvious characteristic of the natural world. Young students need to begin understanding that diversity in nature is essential for natural systems to survive. Students can explore and investigate a pond to learn that different organisms feed on different things (NSES, 1996).

What Concepts Should You Include in Your Curriculum?

The concepts selected as learning objectives for students should be based on your knowledge of the students and of the community in which they live, the nature of the larger society, and the Big Ideas in science. Ask yourself the following questions as you begin to prepare for teaching:

- What experiences have the students had before coming to my class?

- In what things do they show an interest?

- What kinds of knowledge and skills do they need to function safely and effectively in the community in which they live and in the global community to which they belong?

- What will they need to know and be able to do to participate and succeed in the larger society?

- Which of the basic science concepts are relevant to them at this stage of their lives?

Questions such as these should be asked and answered as you develop your plan for teaching science.

Table 6.1 lists the topics selected by Texas, California, and New York State to reflect the national standards. The content standards of these three states closely align to each other and also to the national *Standards,* with an emphasis on inquiry.

	Science Topics Covered by Each Grade,
Table 6.1	**According to California, New York, and Texas Standards**

Grade	California	New York	Texas
3	Physical science; Life science; Earth science; Investigation and experimentation	Matter, energy; Simple machines; Plant and animal adaptations	Natural world: Rocks, soil; Water and atmospheric gases; Change caused by force: Direction and position of objects pushed and pulled; Movement of Earth's surface; Magnetism and gravity; Organisms' needs, habitats, and competition within ecosystems
4	Physical science; Life science; Earth science; Investigation and experimentation	Animals and plants in their environment; Electricity and magnetism; Properties of water; Interactions of air, water, and land	Natural world components and processes: Properties of soil; Effects of oceans on land; Role of sun as major source of energy; Physical properties of matter; Changes in states of matter: Addition/reduction of heat
5	Physical science; Life science; Earth science; Investigation and experimentation	Nature of science; Earth science; Food and nutrition; Exploring ecosystems	Structure and function of Earth systems: Crust, mantle, and core; Effect of weathering on land forms; Past events and effect on present: Growth, erosion, and dissolving; Classification of matter; Magnetism; Physical states; Conductivity; Energy: Light, heat, electricity
6	Focus on Earth science; Investigation and experimentation	Simple and complex machines; Weather; Diversity of life; Interdependence	Components of solar system: Sun, planets, moon, and asteroids; Tilt of Earth and revolution/rotation; Rock cycle and watersheds; Changes in objects when acted on by force; Classification of substances by chemical properties; Interactions between matter and energy: Water cycle and decay; Life processes and relationship between structure and function

Teacher Activity: Your State Standards and Teaching Topics

Locate your state standards and list the topics you are required to teach at your grade level.

Grade _____

Topics that should be covered:	**Your level of comfort (5–1)**
1. _____	_____
2. _____	_____
3. _____	_____
4. _____	_____
5. _____	_____
6. _____	_____

Next to each topic, write your level of comfort, with (5) being most comfortable (you know the content and have appropriate strategies for teaching the topic) and (1) being least comfortable (you need to understand content and develop teaching strategies).

How Do You Build an Effective Science Learning Environment?

This section is informed by the National Science Education program and system standards. You will find additional information at http://www.nap.edu/readingroom/books/nses/.

Creating an adequate environment for science teaching is a shared responsibility. Teachers lead the way in the design and use of resources, but school administrators, students, parents, and community members must meet their responsibility to ensure that the resources are available to be used. Developing a schedule that allows time for science investigations needs the cooperation of all in the school. Acquiring materials requires the appropriation of funds. Maintaining scientific equipment is the shared responsibility of students and teachers alike. Designing appropriate use of the scientific institutions and resources in the local community requires the participation of the school and those institutions and parents, teachers and students.

Time, space, and materials are critical components of an effective science learning environment that promotes sustained inquiry and understanding.

Time

You should structure available time so that students are able to engage in extended investigations. A major difficulty that teachers face, with the emphasis on reading and mathematics skills, is that there is not enough time left in the school day for science. As you plan your day, think of opportunities for integrating reading, mathematics, and writing into your science block. Research shows that the hands-on nature of science can be a place to engage and motivate students to apply literacy and mathematics skills. You can read a book about seeds (reading), have students sow seeds (science), measure the growth of the seedlings (mathematics), and write about the experience (writing). Building scientific understanding takes time on a daily basis and over the long term.

As you begin to plan, see if you can use blocks of time, interdisciplinary strategies, and field experiences to give students many opportunities to engage in serious scientific investigation as an integral part of their science learning. When considering how to structure available time, remember students need time to try out ideas, make mistakes, ponder, and discuss with one another. As you schedule your time, provide adequate blocks of time for students to set up scientific equipment and carry out experiments, to go on field trips, or to reflect and share with each other. Allow your students to work in varied groupings—alone, in pairs, in small groups, as a whole class—and on varied tasks, such as reading, conducting experiments, reflecting, writing, and sharing.

Space

Create a setting for student work that is flexible and supportive of science inquiry. The arrangement of available space and furnishings in the classroom or laboratory influences the nature of the learning that takes place. You need regular, adequate space for science to allow your students to work safely in groups of various sizes at various tasks, to maintain their work in progress, and to display and discuss their results.

Materials

Make the available science tools, materials, media, and technological resources accessible to students. Effective science teaching depends on the availability and organization of materials, equipment, media, and technology. An effective science learning environment requires a broad range of basic scientific materials, as well as specific tools for particular topics and learning experiences. As you plan for teaching you should select the most appropriate materials and make decisions about when, where, and how to make them accessible. Such decisions balance safety, proper use, and availability with the need for students to participate actively in designing experiments, selecting tools, and constructing apparatus, all of which are critical to the development of an understanding of inquiry. It is also important for students to learn how to access scientific information from Websites, books, periodicals, videos, data bases, electronic communication, and people with expert knowledge. As your students seek information you need to help them evaluate and interpret the information they have acquired through those resources. You can find good materials at yard sales, thrift stores, and flea markets, as well as on a walk on the beach or through the woods or just looking around in your own backyard.

Safety

Always ensure a safe working environment. Safety is a fundamental concern when doing science. You must know and apply the necessary safety regulations in the storage, use, and care of the materials used by students. You also need to adhere to safety rules and guidelines that are established by national organizations such as the American Chemical Society (ACS) and the Occupational Safety and Health Administration (OSHA), as well as by local and state regulatory agencies. It is critical that at the beginning, you teach students how to engage safely in investigations inside and outside the classroom. You also need to consider allergic reactions as you plan teaching materials.

Involve Students

Involve young students in designing the learning environment. As part of challenging students to take responsibility for their learning, you could involve them in the design and management of the learning environment. Even the youngest students can and should participate in discussions and decisions about using time and space for work. For example, they can come to consensus about the location of the science corner or the aquarium. With this sharing comes responsibility for care of space and resources. As students pursue their inquiries, they need access to resources and a voice in determining what is needed. The more independently students can access what they need, the more they can take responsibility for their own work. Students are also invaluable in identifying resources beyond the school (NSES, 1996).

How Can You Set Up Your Classroom for Science?

Your physical setting will be dependent on your location, the economics of your community, and the importance that has been placed on science in the school and district. You might be in an urban school in which you cannot leave anything in your classroom and have to bring your supplies in daily, or, at the other extreme, you might be in a very wealthy district or school with a room large enough to accommodate a science center and ongoing experiments. You might even have a room designated to science. Whatever your circumstances, you can teach science. I have watched teachers make science come alive in schools without walls, using materials they pull out of their handbags; I have also seen science taught in classrooms that have better science materials than some teacher training programs.

Here are some ideas of what you can include in your room:

1. **Why board.** This is a prominent board on which you or your students write their "Why" questions.

2. **Science word wall.** Some words to include are: *science, scientists, problem, materials, procedure, observations, animals, plants,* etc. Other words can be added as topics are taught. (For example, a lesson on animals may include the words *living, nonliving, insects,* and *mammals.*)

3. **Science library.** Start collecting science books (fiction and nonfiction). Have students bring in books from their collections to donate to the classroom.

4. **Science materials.** Below is a list of basic science materials. (See *Science Stories* by Janice Koch (2005) for a complete suggested materials list.) You can purchase materials from discount or dollar stores or party stores or check online at www.discountschoolsupply.com or http://edushop. edu4kids.com/catalog/default.php; for a listing of free or inexpensive science resources, check http://amasci.com/edu_free_sci.html or nsta.org.

   • set of hand lenses

   • balance scales

   • measuring cups and spoons (in metric and standard measures)

   • assortment of pine cones, acorns, seeds from different plants

   • animal antlers and bones, fossils, rock collections, and seashells

   • fish bowl with goldfish (No heater needed; the fish live a long time.)

   • rabbits, hamsters, guinea pigs, lizards, or hermit crabs (These pets are easy to take care of, and students love to take them home on vacations.) Remember: Get parental approval first and check with parents about allergies before bringing pets into the classroom.

- ant farm or butterfly garden (Purchase caterpillars in the spring; students can watch them go through metamorphosis.)
- basic cooking supplies (salt, sugar, cooking oil, baking soda, flour)
- containers (beakers, bottles, plastic cups, funnels)
- Epsom salts (used to show scientific concepts like evaporation, dissolving, texture)
- other supplies—potting soil, balloons, drinking straws, scale, flashlights, string, magnets, thermometers

5. **Science corner.** A science corner is a special interactive corner in the classroom devoted to science where

- science materials are located
- there is usually a large table for working
- the materials on the table are well organized so that items are accessible
- both formal and informal science teaching and learning can take place

Teacher Activity: Science Corners

Science corners should be changed often to meet the needs of the students and the curriculum. Your science corner should focus on encouraging learning through discovery. Science corners are not only the responsibility of the teacher. Students can also

- contribute items to the science corner
- participate in taking care of a science corner in their classroom
- rotate as the designated "science resource person" in charge of the corner

Before setting up your science corner, and as part of your plan for teaching, answer the following questions:

- What do you see as the value of a science corner?

_____

- How would you utilize a science corner in your classroom?

_____

- What materials and resources would you include?

_____

- Where can you find materials for science teaching?

_____

(continued on next page)

Teacher Activity: Science Corners (continued)

● Do you have a budget for science materials?

_____

● What is the budget? Who purchases materials?

_____

● How many months in advance do you need your list of required materials?

_____

● Are there science kits available in your school?

_____

● Is there a science room or closet with materials from previous years?

_____

If you do not know the answers to some of these questions, you should talk to your principal. You need this information as you begin to plan for teaching.

Teacher Activity: Final Reflection

Many of you teach science in a "regular" classroom. As you develop your plan for teaching science, think about the following:

● How can you adapt your current classroom to create an effective science learning environment?
● What do you need to change or add to your room to accommodate science teaching?
● Would you have to change your teaching schedule? Can you change it?
● What issues arise in science that might not occur in your other subject areas?
● Where can you store your science materials?

Take-Away Thought

When your students come to you in the third grade, they have emerged as scientists. Between the third and fifth grade, they become budding scientists.

7

Resources You Can Use in Your Science Teaching

Focus Questions

- What resources are available for teaching grades 3–5 science?

- Where can you find information on these resources?

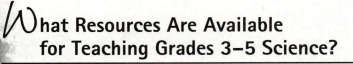

What Resources Are Available for Teaching Grades 3–5 Science?

The school science program must extend beyond the walls of the school to the resources of the community. Your students' education should not be limited to what goes on within the walls of the school building. The classroom is a limited environment. As an effective teacher, you should identify and use resources outside the school. The physical environment in and around the school can be used as a living laboratory for the study of natural phenomena. Whether your school is located in a densely populated urban area, a sprawling suburb, a small town, or a rural area, the environment can and should be used as a resource for science study. Working with others in your school and with the community, you can build these resources into your work with students.

In this exercise, explore the science teaching resources that are available for use in your day-to-day teaching.

Teacher Activity: Your Available Resources for Teaching Science

List the resources you think you will have available for teaching science.

_____

_____

_____

_____

_____

_____

_____

_____

_____

_____

_____

Let us take a look at some of the available resources for teaching science to grades 3–5 students.

You

The first and most critical resource that you have for teaching science is you—your willingness to be adventurous, to be flexible, and to use everything around you as a science teaching resource for your students. Science is a difficult subject to teach, and you need to gather all the resources you can find to help you in your teaching of science that students will find meaningful and that does not stifle their endless "why" questions. When they leave you and move up to the next level, their scientific selves must continue to emerge.

For many elementary teachers, science is an entity they do not know or feel confident about; neither do they know how to reply to all the questions that students pose to them. As teachers, we sometimes feel that we are supposed to have all the answers. I vividly recall one class during my graduate work, when I was preparing to be a science teacher, when my K–6 methods professor wrote on the board the following: "Wait time" and "I do not know. Let's find out." He proceeded to tell us that these would be the strategies we would use most frequently in our daily teaching. He was so correct. As a teacher, I have found that I am most successful if I give my students time to reflect before responding to my questions and if I foster an environment in my class in which I work with students to find answers to their questions rather than supplying them with the answer. I did not have to be an expert at science to teach it effectively. We learn together. Students become the masters of their own learning. Throughout this book, there are strategies you can use to help your students find answers to their "why" questions. You want to give the students the best start in life. In the early years, you want them to begin to develop critical thinking and life skills. These are the skills that are basic in the development of scientific literacy. Good science education fosters scientific literacy, which in turn equates to critical thinking. As their first teacher, you have the development of their critical thinking capacity in your hands. However, you are not alone. The following sections explore the resources you can use to assist you in this task.

Scientists

If we want our students to become scientists, we need to provide them with role models so that they can begin from an early age to identify with scientists and to realize that they too can aspire to being a scientist. Our nation's communities have many specialists, including those in transportation, health care delivery, communications, computer technologies, music, art, cooking, mechanics, and many other fields that have scientific aspects. Specialists often are available as resources for classes and for individual students. Many communities have access to science centers and museums as well as to the science communities in higher education, national laboratories, and industry. These resources can contribute greatly to the understanding of science and encourage students to further their interests outside of school.

You are working with young students, and this is the time when you should begin to have them interact with scientists, to think about careers in science, and to begin to find answers to questions such as:

- What do scientists do?
- Who are scientists?
- What do scientists look like?
- What does it feel like to be a scientist?

This is when you should begin to bring scientists from the community into the classroom and expose your students to the day-to-day life of a scientist. You want students to begin to realize that scientists are normal people, scientists are "cool." This is the age when students begin to talk about what they want to be when they grow up, and you want them to include "being a scientist" as one of their aspirations. They can begin to think about being a nurse, pharmacist, doctor, dentist, medical technician, laboratory researcher, physicist, chemist, environmental scientist. Remember: one way of having students include these images in their dreams is to expose them to real-life role models.

Teacher Activity: Scientists in Your Community

1. Make a list of the scientists you would like to come to your classroom. Include their contact information and what you perceive they can contribute to your students. You can use your local yellow pages or the Web to locate them.

Name	Contact information	Scientific contribution
_____	_____	_____
_____	_____	_____
_____	_____	_____
_____	_____	_____
_____	_____	_____

2. Once you have completed this list, have your students write the questions they would like to ask the scientist on their question board. Have the scientists answer those questions during their visit to your class.

Nonformal Institutions

The world outside of the classroom can provide useful stimuli for responding to questions your students have asked and for getting them to ask new questions. Schools are essentially places that provide the opportunity for intense, conscious, systematic, and formalized learning. The following guidelines for visits to these institutions were originally generated by the U.S. DoE. For additional information you should consult their Website: http://www.ed.gov/pubs/ parents/science/index.html. You should also visit the Website: http://www.yal-laa.com/directory/reference/museums/science/ of the education programs listed in the references for site opportunities and guidelies for your grade level.

Nonformal science settings provide your students with opportunities to develop their scientific literacy outside the walls of the school. Nonformal sites that encompass unique settings include the following:

- museums
- zoos
- botanical gardens
- rivers
- parks
- playgrounds

In such settings, information, stimulation, and experiences are provided almost entirely through objects, their interpretative display, and, in many cases, the manipulation of these objects. If activities at these sites are well structured, they can go a long way toward providing your students with levels of knowledge and awareness in science to help them meet the requirements of the *NSES* and the *benchmarks*. You can use field trips to connect to the national and state standards, the Big Ideas, and your curriculum. Your field trip should extend and reinforce what is taking place in your classroom. Nonformal sites, with their abundance of resources, provide opportunities to reinforce the formalized learning of the school system with concrete experiences. They can present phenomena in the form of exhibits that are interactive, with a focus on enabling visitors to explore, manipulate, and experiment. They provide a venue for your students to see animals or plants that you talk about in school or that they see in books or TV. You can include in your curriculum visits to museums, zoos, parks, botanical gardens, and even to the area around your school. Try to focus on science around you and use the environment to teach science. Remember science can be learned in many places and environments.

Zoos. Almost all students enjoy a trip to the zoo. We can use zoos to encourage their interest in the natural world and to introduce them to animal diversity.

Guessing games can help students understand structure and function. Here are some sample questions:

- Why do you think the seal has flippers? (The seal uses flippers to swim through the water.)

- Why do you think the gibbons have such long and muscular arms? (Their arms help them swing through the trees.)

- Why does the armadillo have a head that looks like it's covered with armor, as well as a body that's covered with small, bony plates? (The armor and plates protect it from being attacked by predators.)

- Why is the snake the same brown color as the ground on which it spends most of its time? (As snakes evolved, the brown ones did not get eaten as quickly.)

Students can learn about organization by seeing related animals. Here are some ideas:

- Have them compare the sizes, legs, feet, ears, claws, feathers, or scales of various animals.

- Ask such questions as: Does the lion look like a regular cat? How are they the same? or Does the gorilla look like the baboon?

Planning a trip to the zoo for a class of twenty-five third- to fifth-graders can be a daunting experience but it is manageable and can be lots of fun for you and your students. Here are a few suggestions to help make your visit worthwhile:

1. **Discuss expectations with your students ahead of time.** What do they think they'll find at the zoo? Very young or insecure students may go to the zoo with a more positive attitude if they are assured that it has food stands, water fountains, and bathrooms.

2. **Don't try to see everything in one visit.** Zoos are such busy places that they can overwhelm youngsters.

3. **Try to visit zoos at off times or hours.** Visiting in winter, for example, or very early in the morning provides some peace and quiet and gives students unobstructed views of the animals. Always visit the zoo before taking your class. Carefully plan what animals you want students to observe.

4. **Look for special exhibits and facilities for students.** Such exhibits as family learning labs or petting zoos provide students the opportunity to touch and examine animals and engage in projects specially designed for them. At some museums children can learn about dinosaurs by engaging in a dinosaur dig. This is often a very engaging and fun activity.

5. **Plan follow-up activities and projects.** A student who particularly liked the flamingos and ducks may enjoy building a bird house for the back yard. One who liked the mud turtle may enjoy using a margarine tub as a base

to a papier-mâché turtle. One who enjoyed the fish might want to start a classroom aquarium.

Museums. Museums are designed today to interest visitors of all ages. Science and technology museums, natural history museums, and students' museums can be found in many middle-sized and smaller communities such as Toledo (Ohio), Monsey (New York), and Worland (Wyoming), as well as in large metropolitan areas like Los Angeles, Chicago, and New York City.

Museums vary in quality. If possible, seek out those that provide opportunities for hands-on activities. Look for museums with

- levers to pull
- bubbles to blow
- lights to switch on
- buttons to push
- animals to stroke
- experiments to do

Natural history museums sometimes have hands-on rooms where students can stroke everything from lizards to Madagascan hissing cockroaches.

Many museums offer special science classes. Look for omni theaters. These enable visitors to see movies projected on a giant screen on subjects ranging from space launches to rafting on the Amazon. The sounds and sights of the experience are extremely realistic and appealing to young students.

If you are unfamiliar with museums in your area, consult a librarian, the Yellow Pages of your telephone book, a local guidebook, or the local newspapers, which often list special exhibits; of course, you can also check their Website pages online. In the references section for this chapter, there is a list of Websites for national museums. You can even take your students for a virtual visit to some museums; for example, the American Museum of Natural History in New York has a Website that takes you through their exhibits.

The tips for visiting the zoo are also helpful when you visit museums or other community facilities.

Aquariums. Aquariums enable youngsters to see everything from starfish to electric eels. Students particularly enjoy feeding times. Remember to call ahead to find out when the penguins, sharks, and other creatures get fed. Check for special shows with sea lions and dolphins.

Farms. A visit to a farm makes a wonderful field trip for young students. It can provide experiences in life science and technology If you don't know a farmer, call the closest 4-H Club, your Cooperative Extension, or a master gardener for a referral. Consider dairy farms as well as vegetable, poultry, pig, and tree farms.

On a dairy farm, students can see cows close up, view silos, and learn what cows eat. Your students can find out from the farmer answers to such questions as:

- Up to what age do calves drink only milk?

- When do they add other items to their diets? What are they?

- Why are the various foods a cow eats nutritious?

A visit to a farm also enables students to identify the difference between calves, heifers, and cows; to watch the cows being milked; to see farm equipment; to sit on tractors; and to ask questions about how tractors work.

If you visit a vegetable farm, encourage your students to look at the crops and ask questions about how they grow. Let them discover what farmers do with their organic waste. Is there a composter on site? How does it work? If your students grew up in an urban area, they may have no idea what apples or potatoes or beans look like growing in a field.

Where Can You Find Information on These Resources?

Science learning and, ultimately, scientific literacy for all depend on the teaching that occurs both in schools and in nonformal settings. As we move toward the attainment of scientific literacy for all, it is imperative that we recognize and utilize the media, industry, education programs, nonformal science centers, museums, and other science learning outlets as valuable segments of our nation's science education infrastructure. As an elementary teacher, you need to develop the ability to use the nonformal context to teach elementary science. These sites can provide immense support as you implement your science teaching in schools that have a paucity of resources but that are located close to nonformal sites that house an abundant, often untapped, set of resources. Here are examples of nonformal institutions you can use as a resource in your teaching. The listing also includes some international sites you might find useful in your science teaching. Visit these Websites to get information about their education programs.

Teacher Activity: Nonformal Resources

1. List the accessible nonformal institutions within walking distance or close proximity of your school. Include their contact information and what you perceive they can contribute to your students:

   _____

   _____

   _____

   _____

   _____

   _____

2. List the nonformal institutions that will accommodate grades 3–5 students:

   _____

   _____

   _____

   _____

   _____

   _____

3. Investigate and list what you need to do to take your students to the site:

   _____

   _____

   _____

   _____

   _____

4. What do these sites offer your students?

   _____

   _____

   _____

   _____

5. Contact these institutions and get their brochures or visit their Websites. Keep all this information in your folder, as you will need to refer to it as you develop your plan for teaching.

Parents

Parents are the first teachers of their children and usually are very keen on being involved in their education. You need to foster their desire to continue this involvement and invite them into the classroom or on field trips. They are the major influences on their students during their early years, so you want them to be involved in and excited about what you are doing in school. Plan family science nights in which you share with them the activities you are doing with their children. Do some activities with them. Have them relive the excitement of discovery. Use parents or community members as judges for your science fairs. This shows students that their parents and the community value science education and builds good school-family relationships.

Invite the community to have your students visit places around the community that use science (dry cleaners, restaurants, hair salons, water department, parks, etc.). When students see science in places they frequent, they will have a better grasp of the importance of science in their daily lives. They will begin to realize that science surrounds them and is worthwhile. Parents and members of the community are usually more than willing to come into the classroom and bring an experiment or talk to the students about science in their lives.

Teacher Activity: Parents as Resources

On the first day of school, or earlier, if practical, send a letter out to parents telling them about what you want to do in science and enlisting their help. Ask for volunteers for field trips, classroom visits, science nights, and other activities you have planned.

Sample Letter to Parents

Dear Parents or Guardians:

Welcome to third grade. My name is _____ and I am excited about the upcoming school year and the possibilities for learning that await my new class.

This is an important time for the academic and social development of your students. This year, we will be spending a considerable amount of time working on their reading, writing, and math skills. Additionally, we will be exploring the world of social studies and science with discussions, readings, activities, and experiments. My goal is to help your student develop a love of learning through exploration of their interests and further development/improvement of their skills in all areas of curriculum.

You will be receiving monthly updates about what your student is learning in class. Additionally, you may receive notes about important events or activities throughout the year.

(continued on next page)

Teacher Activity: Parents as Resources (continued)

In order to make this year successful, not only does your student need your support at home, but also in the classroom. I would like to enhance the learning experience with a number of hands-on activities and experiments in science. If you have any supplies at home that you could donate from the suggested list below, or anything else you think we could use, please send them in with your student or drop them off at the front desk with room number _____ on the front.

- *glue*
- *scissors*
- *string*
- *butcher paper*
- *magnets*
- *boxes*
- *quick-growing seeds*
- *leaves/plants*
- *cups (paper/plastic)*
- *small mirrors*
- *plastic bags*
- *empty bottles (soda, juice)*
- *plastic spoons*
- *aquarium*
- *fossils*
- *rocks*

I would like to thank you in advance for your help. This is going to be a great year. I look forward to meeting both you and your sudent this fall. Please do not hesitate to contact me by email or phone if you have any questions or other concerns.

Sincerely,

_____

Note: The list of materials needed will vary, based on the needs of your school district.

Use parents' responses to your letter to make up your database of available parents, and remember to enlist their help as you teach science. You should include their name, address, phone numbers, expertise, and availability. You can also ask them if they are available to accompany the class on field trips.

Journals and Books

You can examine the following journals for interesting activities that will engage your emerging scientists:

- *Science and Children* (National Science Teachers' Association; NSTA)
- *Journal of Elementary Science Education* (JESE)

As a teacher, you should consider membership in NSTA, since this association provides numerous teaching resources and activities through their journals, Website, wikis, and national and regional meetings.

Here are three books that you may want to add to your resource collection:

1. *Ten-Minute Field Trips* (3rd ed.) by Helen Ross Russell (1998).
2. *Teaching Green—The Elementary Years: Hands-On Learning in Grades K–5* edited by Tim Grant and Gail Littlejohn (2005).
3. *Into the Field: A Guide to Locally Focused Teaching* by Leslie Clare Walker (2005).

Internet

The Internet has evolved into an excellent resource for teaching science. You can find useful ideas for teaching science at all levels. Web resources promote:

- active learning
- more hands-on experiences
- creativity
- engaged students
- enhanced lessons

An excellent Website is TeachersTV.com, a British-based site that provides content, activities, strategies, and useful teaching tips for K–12 science.

Tables 7.1 and 7.2 list Websites helpful for planning activities for teaching grades 3–5 science.

Teacher Activity: Integrating the Web into Your Teaching

Science content for your grade

Grade 3

_____

_____

_____

_____

_____

Grade 4

_____

_____

_____

_____

_____

Grade 5

_____

_____

_____

_____

_____

Relevant websites that contain materials you can use

_____

_____

_____

_____

_____

_____

_____

_____

_____

_____

_____

_____

_____

_____

_____

Table 7.1 General Websites for Any Grade, Children and Teachers

- Exploratorium Website—Live webcasts, with scientists and museum tour guides
  http://www.exploratorium.edu/index.html

- Website with small useful science modules on a variety of science topics
  http://www.bbc.co.uk/schools/

- Magic School Bus virtual tours
  http://place.scholastic.com/magicschoolbus/tour/home.htm

- Foss Website—Each module has information on the topics: pictures, other websites,
  movies, and interactive games for kids as well as parent-teacher information
  http://www.fossweb.com/modulesK–2/index.html

- Brain Pop—videos and quizzes on science topics
  http://www.brainpop.com/science/seeall/

- For teachers—lets you customize your grade and subject and it gives you a list of
  great resources
  http://www.pbs.org/teachers/sciencetech/

- Bill Nye's interactive Website
  http://www.billnye.com/

- British-based Website— TeachersTV.com

Source: This list was developed by two NYC elementary teachers, Hallie Saltz and Lindsey Webster, using materials modified from *Teaching Science as Investigation* by Richard H. Moyer, Jay. K. Hackett, and Susan A. Everett (Upper Saddle River, NJ: Prentice Hall, 2006).

$\mathcal{T}able\ 7.2$ Suggested Websites for Use in Grades 3–5

Unit 1

1. Matter: What are observable and measurable properties of matter?

1. Bones Games: http://www.studentssmuseum.org/games/grades_3-5.htm

2. Exploring the Temperate Deciduous Forest: How are plants and animals in the ecosystem connected?

2. What you need to survive: combinations of food, water, exercise, and rest: http://www.bbc.co.uk/schools/scienceclips/ages6_7/health_growth.shtml

3. Healthy Body: Heart and Lungs: You are what you eat.

3. Rebuild the skeleton: http://www.fossweb.com/modules3-6/HumanBody/index.html
http://place.scholastic.com/magicschoolbus/tour/tous.htm?body

Unit 2

1. Energy: How do different forms of energy interact with matter and with each other (sound and light)?

1. Sound-building an orchestra: http://www.carnegiehall.org/article/explore_and_learn/art_online_resources_listening_adventures.html

2. Interaction of Air, Water, and Land: What forces affect our land, city, and planet?

2. See, find, learn, and get a clue about recycling: http://www.epa.gov/recyclecity

3. Healthy Planet: Clean air and water, waste management.

3. Earth Day: http://funschool.kaboose.com/formula-fusion/games/game_earth_day.html
Soil lab: http://school.discovery.com/schooladventures/soil/index.html

Unit 3

1. The Sun, Earth, and Moon System: How do atmospheric factors affect the seasons?

1. Solar Energy: http://www.fossweb.com/modules3-6/SolarEnergy/index.html

2. Forces and Work: How do forces affect the motion of objects (gravity, friction)?

2. Experiment with different amounts of friction: http://www.bbc.co.uk/schools/ks2bitesize/science/activities/friction.shtml
Videos about gravity, space, and collisions: http://teacher.scholastic.com/activities/explorations/space/scholasticspace
Levers and Pulleys: http://www.fossweb.com/modules3-6/LeversandPulleys/index.html

(continued on next page)

Table 7.2   Suggested Websites for Use in Grades 3–5 (continued)

Unit	Websites
Unit 3 (continued)	
3. Healthy Planet II: Sources of Energy (sun, fossil fuels, conserving energy).	3. Making the earth orbit around the sun: http://www.bbc.co.uk/schools/ks2bitesize/science/activities/earth_sun_moon.shtml
Unit 4	
1. Plant & Animal Characteristics and Behavior: What are the structures and functions of plants/animals, and how do they function in various ecosystems?	1. Learn which factors are important for survival: http://www.fossweb.com/modules3-6/Environments/index.html Learn about seeds and fruits. Get to know crayfish, their structures, and behaviors: http://www.fossweb.com/modules3-6/StructuresofLife/index.html Life cycle and structures of plants: http://www.bbc.co.uk/schools/ks2bitesize/science/activities/life_cycles.shtml
2. Electricity and Magnetism: How can energy be used?	2. Simple circuits: make the bulb grow more brightly: http://www.bbc.co.uk/schools/ks2bitesize/science/activities/changing_circuits.shtml Forces: http://www.bbc.co.uk/schools/ks2bitesize/science/activities/forces_action.shtml
3. Healthy Planet III: Marine Studies.	
Unit 5	
1. Genetics and Heredity: How and why do living things look and act the way they do?	
2. Human Impact on the Environment: Staying Healthy.	2. Exercise and nutrition: http://www.bbc.co.uk/schools/ks2bitesize/science/activities/keeping_healthy.shtml
3. Impact of Technology: Humans on the environment, inventions.	

Source: Adapted from: *Teaching Science as Investigations,* by Richard H. Moyer, Jay K. Hackett, and Susan A. Everett (Upper Saddle River, NJ: Prentice Hall, 2006), by two New York City elementary teachers, Hallie Saltz and Lindsey Webster.

Education Programs

Many institutions have extensive Websites and offer virtual fieldtrips that can be integrated into your teaching. In this chapter's references, you will find a listing of some of these programs.

Take-Away Thought

Resources for teaching science are everywhere. You just need to know where to look.
Do not use lack of money as an excuse for not teaching science.

Developing Your Plan for Teaching Science

Focus Questions

- Where am I in my development as a science teacher?

- Where am I going in my science teaching practice?

- How do I plan to be an effective science teacher?

- How will I know when I have arrived at my best level of practice?

As you progress through the exercises and activities in this chapter and begin to plan learning experiences for your students, you should be developing an awareness of your own level of preparedness for the task ahead.

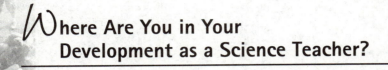

Where Are You in Your Development as a Science Teacher?

Initial Reflection: Assessing Where You Are

Whatever your role in science teaching, these are some questions to think about as you develop the phases of your plan for each lesson within your curriculum.

1. Under what conditions do you currently teach (or plan to teach) science?

   _____

2. Is your curriculum text or kit based? Or a combination of both?

   _____

3. Has your school district adopted a specific curriculum?

   _____

4. Has your school developed its own curriculum?

   _____

5. Has your school adopted a specific textbook?

   _____

6. Are you expected to use the textbook as written?

   _____

7. Are you expected to develop your own curriculum?

   _____

8. Do you have a science cluster teacher (or a teacher specifically dedicated to science teaching)?

   _____

Earlier, we used the analogy of going on a journey. To continue that analogy if you do not know where you are then it is difficult to plan your future journey to your final destination. While answering the question, "Where am I in my development as a science teacher?" you should ask and seek answers to the question, "Where are my students?" Consider these questions:

- What do you need to do to prepare all your students for the journey to scientific literacy?
- What is the range of intellectual abilities in the class?
- What about their emotional development?
- What do they currently know?
- What did they do in the previous grade?
- What experiences do they bring from home?

Remember that in your class you will have different intellectual abilities, as well as significant differences in emotional and motor skill development.

Where Are You Going in Your Science Teaching Practice?

Each state has interpreted the national *Standards* and the *Benchmarks* to develop their own state standards and frameworks. In turn, many districts have developed their own standards, which are often translated into individual school standards. (See Figure 8.1.) These are the standards that you use in your own classroom when you begin teaching to achieve scientific literacy for all of your children.

Figure 8.1   The *Standards* and the *Benchmarks*

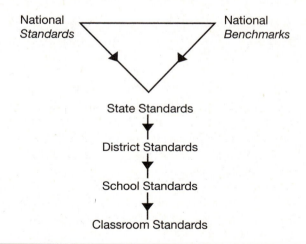

National *Standards* National *Benchmarks*

State Standards

District Standards

School Standards

Classroom Standards

All of the previous chapters have been leading up to this one in which you plan for the journey to scientific literacy for all your students. The information you collected in chapters 1 through 7 are essential for planning to teach science in your classroom. In your planning, you need to decide which conditions are most conducive to learning in your contextual framework. Remember, there is no single format or strategy that meets the needs of all communities and the teaching and learning styles of all teachers and students. You have the opportunity to develop your own format based on the needs of your students and your ability to meet those needs. No curriculum developer can produce the optimum teaching strategy for your classroom. Only you can do this.

As you develop your curriculum, you should assimilate ideas presented in this book, in curriculum material you have seen, and in Websites and in material developed by your state or elsewhere. Collect and use as many resources as you can find and then adapt them to make your own curriculum for use in your current classroom. Remember also that your plans must always be flexible, since you do not know what questions will surface as you engage your students in new experiences. Their questions and interest might take your lesson in a completely different direction. Always be prepared for the unpredictable. You should be constantly engaged in the task of decision making as you sift, sort, and decide on meaningful experiences for your students.

State Standards

In Appendix 1, you will find the *National Science Education Standards* and the *Benchmarks*. These are the guides that each state uses to make decisions about the content of their K–12 science requirements.

Locate the national *Standards* and copy them for your personal use. You should store them in your folder. Go to this Website: http://www.nap.edu/readingroom/books/nses/overview.html#organization.

Teacher Activity: Mapping the State Standards

1. Go to your state Website. Find the state standards for grades 3–5 (sometimes called frameworks) and include them in your folder. If you have problems locating your state Website, you can check http://edstandards.org/standards.html. (This site, developed by Charles Hill, has been on the Internet since August 1995, first with the Putnam Valley School District, and now the Wappingers Central School District, both in upstate New York.)

2. Review both national and state standards for similarities and differences. Are there any major differences? Does one reflect the other?

In your folder you now have the National Standards, the benchmarks and your state standards. Study these documents carefully and see if you can make connections between them. Read the documents and highlight key words that point to the need for activity-based instruction. Explore your state, district, or city Websites for science lessons and activities.

City and District Standards

As you research further, you will find that many cities and districts have developed their own standards or scope and sequence. For example, New York City recently developed a scope and sequence for K–8.

Teacher Activity: Mapping the District Standards

Go to your district Website, find the relevant standards, and include them in your folder.

School Standards

Teacher Activity: Mapping Your School Standards

Go to your school Website, find the relevant standards, and include them in your folder.

EXAMPLE OF SCHOOL STANDARDS

Here is an example of what standards one suburban school recommends for use in 3–5 science.

1. **Grade 3**
   - Identify the life cycles of plants and animals.
   - Analyze changes in plants and animals and ways they survive.
   - Evaluate how forms of energy affect matter.
   - Synthesize how heat energy moves, changes matter, and is measured.
   - Differentiate between advantages and disadvantages of various energy sources.
   - Create a model of the water cycle.
   - Identify the effects of pollution and methods of conservation.

2. **Grade 4**

- Identify the basic needs of animals and their adaptations.
- Classify living things.
- Identify characteristics of different animal groups.
- Describe properties of magnets and forms of electrical energy.
- Construct electrical circuits.
- Explain sources of electrical current.
- Identify properties and uses of minerals and rocks.
- Analyze elements and forces of the Earth's structure.

3. **Grade 5**

- Identify the parts of flowering plants and explain various plant processes.
- Compare and classify plants according to specialized cells and structures.
- Describe specific structural adaptations of plants.
- Explain and describe properties of light and sound.
- Describe the function of lenses and their uses.
- Analyze the effect of light on color.
- Explain the hearing process.
- Identify methods of controlling, recording, identifying, and transmitting sound.
- Describe various tools used by astronomers.
- Illustrate the structure of the solar system and identify the properties of stars and galaxies.

You now have a large folder containing the national, state, district, and your school standards; examples of activities and addresses for numerous Websites where you can find additional activities. Do you now feel more knowledgeable about what needs to be taught?

Classroom Standards

In your classroom, you make final decisions as to what science will be taught. You are in control of what curriculum is enacted in your classroom and how it will be taught; your teaching is framed by who you are. You have the responsibility to teach science that will foster interest, participation, and achievement in science. So far you have collected the national, state, and your school standards. Now what? How do you convert all this information to your classroom teaching? How do you foster relationships with other teachers, mentors, administrators, parents, and community members to enhance your science teaching? As we progress through this book, we will begin to put together the parts of your science curriculum for your grade level. We will work on creating a curriculum for your day-to-day teaching that is compliant with standards and relevant to your students' personal context.

Now that you have collected information on what has to be learned, begin to think about developing meaningful science learning experiences.

How Do You Plan to Be an Effective Science Teacher?

This question is probably the most open-ended of the four questions. The students have ideas about the natural world; your task is to discover and identify these ideas. Your destination has been determined by the national standards and benchmarks. Even though the answer to the question "How do I get there?" might be provided in curricular materials, you will still need to consider the appropriateness of the suggested sequence of procedures, the proposed modes of instruction, the organization of students, and the selection and management of materials. You still need to plan for what happens in your classroom on a day-to-day basis.

Beginning the Plan

Consider the following guidelines, which were partially informed by the DoE (1991).

1. What works best for young students
   - Young students learn science best and understand scientific ideas better if they are able to investigate and experiment.
   - Hands-on science can also help students think critically and gain confidence in their own ability to solve problems.
   - What engages young students? Things they can see, touch, manipulate, modify; situations that allow them to figure out what happens; events and puzzles they can investigate—in short, the very stuff of science.
   - Hands-on science can be messy and time consuming. Before you get started, see what is involved in an activity, including required materials and how long the activity might take.
   - Less Is More: The best way to help students learn to think scientifically is to introduce them to just a few topics in depth.

2. Finding the right activity for your class
   - Different students have different interests and need different science projects. A butterfly collection that was a big hit with a nine-year-old girl may not be a big hit with her twin brother.

- Knowing your students is the best way to find suitable activities. Encourage activities that are neither too hard nor too easy. If in doubt, err on the easy side, since something too difficult may give the idea that science itself is too hard.

- Age suggestions on book jackets or games are just that—suggestions. They may not reflect the interest or ability of the student. A student who is interested in a subject can often handle material for a higher age group, while a student who is not interested in or has not been exposed to the subject may need to start with something for a younger age group.

- Consider a student's personality, learning style, and social skills. Some projects are best done alone, others in a group; some require help, others require little or no supervision. Some students like to work alone or in a diad, while others prefer large group work.

- Select activities appropriate for the student's environment. A brightly lighted city isn't the best place for star gazing; you might consider a trip to a planetarium or having a travelling planetarium in your class. If you are in a suburban or rural area, you can consider star-gazing activities with family involvement.

- Allow your students to help select the activities. If you don't know whether Stacy would rather collect shells or grow beans, ask her. When she picks something she wants to do, she will learn more and have a better time doing it.

3. Becoming a scientist

- The elementary school is a good place to start teaching students scientific ethics. You should tell them how important it is to be accurate about their observations and measurements.

- Students need to know it's all right to make mistakes; we all make mistakes, and we can learn from them. Explain that important discoveries are made only if we are willing and able to correct our mistakes.

- Help your students understand that it is important to find out for themselves.

Rationale for Teaching a Topic

Why should your students be expected to demonstrate the desired behavior in your lesson or activity? As students progress through school and through their science classes, one of the most frequently asked question is "Why do I have to study this?" You must know why you are teaching and what you are teaching and clearly communicate this to your students. For example, you are teaching safety procedures during a field trip because you are taking your class to visit the zoo, and each student needs to know how to be safe while at the zoo. Or your students are learning about the parts of a seed because next week they will begin a class project on "Growing Your Own Salad."

$\mathcal{T}$eacher $\mathcal{A}$ctivity: Setting Goals for Teaching a Lesson

Answer these questions as you do your lesson planning:

- What am I hoping my students will get out of this science experience?

- What science concepts do I want to help them develop?

- What should my students be able to do as a result of their interactions in this science experience?

- What materials and procedures will be most conducive to the desired behaviors?

- How will I engage my students in the experience?

- What will my students learn from this experience?

- What degree of mastery of learning should my students demonstrate?

If you use the questions as a guide as you plan for instruction, they can serve as the compass, or global positioning system (GPS), for your journey, always keeping you on the right path.

As you plan your route, here are some things to consider:

- Where are your students in relation to the goals of the lesson?

- Given the physical constraints of the classroom and the presence or absence of equipment, can your students achieve the goal for your lesson?

- Remember that your students bring to your lesson all sorts of entry behaviors and existing understandings and misunderstandings which will determine how they relate to the goal you have for the lesson.

- What individual differences exist among your students in terms of their abilities to achieve the goal? What similarities are there?

Once you develop a better understanding of where your students are in relation to the goals, you can more accurately predict the amount of time they'll need to achieve it.

As you specify what you expect students to do, remember to use terms that can be readily observed. This will help you better recognize the behavior and know that your students are performing adequately. Some of these terms can include: *arrange, classify, compare, construct, list, measure, organize, select.* These terms are extremely important and become the pivotal component of your instruction. They help you to answer the question "What should my students be able to do as a result of interacting with the materials I have provided?"

Deciding on Your Mode of Science Instruction

This is probably the most exciting part of planning. This is where you can demonstrate your creativity and imagination. You have limitless resources from which to select. Here are some possibilities in your classroom:

- hands-on inquiry
- involvement of students in investigating materials then talking about what they have discovered
- technology-based lessons involving heavy emphasis on computers, probes, smart boards, Websites, etc.
- project-based learning
- readings by the teacher, the students, or both
- short lecture by the teacher, or lecture combined with materials and demonstration
- science corners for self-directed learning
- "science share sessions" by the students
- games or simulation activities
- field trips—away from, near, or on the school grounds
- pantomimes, plays, and other dramatizations
- scientists in the classroom
- interviews

These are just a few of the possibilities. Your selection of any one mode or a combination of several depends on your instructional objective for the lesson and the type of technology to which you have access. Which instructional mode will best help your students achieve the intended goal? Remember that the repeated use of one mode of instruction over a long period of time can eventually lose its appeal. You need variety to spice up your science class and to maintain the interest of your students.

Organizing Your Class

You also need to consider lessons designed for the total class, for small groups, or for individuals. Class size can range from under ten students to thirty or more. If you are in a school system in which small classes exist, your instructional strategies will be very different from systems in which the class size is over thirty. Using small groups can provide students with opportunities for sharing, discussing, and cooperative learning.

As students engage in small groups, they develop skills of self-control and self-discipline, which are necessary social skills. Small groups also provide the opportunity for young students to have an active, personal, and direct involvement in their own learning process; to express their creativity; and to begin to realize that they can learn independently of their teacher. There are many advantages to small group work, but it is also very difficult to arrange successfully. Do not be discouraged if it does not work the first time around. Keep persisting, since the advantages outweigh the disadvantages.

Selecting and Managing Materials

Effective science encounters for students involve their interacting with materials—more specifically, with real objects from the natural world. Whenever possible, use real objects in your science classroom. Selecting what you hope will be the most meaningful learning materials for your students is a crucial task. You can complete all the mental preparations for presenting a meaningful science encounter and then see your efforts fizzle because the materials you selected were meaningless, ineffective, or mishandled.

Here are some issues that the U.S. DoE has suggested that you consider as you select learning materials for your class:

1. **Safety.** Avoid objects that might be harmful to the students. Be prepared for breaks, spills, and stains. If objects are to be tasted or smelled, first check the students' records for information on allergies or other susceptibilities. Small animals such as hamsters or butterflies should be handled cautiously.

2. **Materials.** Balances should balance; microscopes should magnify; magnets should attract magnetic materials; wheels on axles should turn. Test materials before use in the classroom; if they do not work, then change your activity. Also, try to have a sufficient quantity of materials so that all your students will have an adequate supply. Young students generally cannot handle relatively small or large objects easily. Most young students are not hesitant to use materials, but a few may shy away from objects that look very fragile or overly complicated.

3. **Timing.** As you arrange and manage your materials, you need to consider timing. When should the students actually have the materials in their hands? When should the materials be visible? Should they have them at the very beginning of the lesson? Remember, young students are more interested in interacting with materials than with the spoken or printed word. So if it is important that something be said or read first, do not distribute the materials until this is done. If necessary, keep the materials out of sight. This strategy also allows the students to give their undivided attention to the materials when they are distributed.

4. **Distribution of materials.** Develop any workable technique that will let you distribute the materials to the class easily and quickly. Much valuable time can be wasted if materials are distributed carelessly. You might try packaging the items, or arranging supply centers in various sections of the room, or appointing certain students as helpers.

5. **Location of use.** Decide in advance where the students are to use the materials, and anticipate the consequences. Prepare for the inevitable; students tend to become more excited or even unruly when interacting with materials on a floor area or outdoors than when seated at desks or around tables. Establish your "rules of engagement" with materials, and make sure that your students understand and obey these rules always.

6. **Need for familiarity time with materials before activity.** Remember that your students need some initial time to explore and handle the materials within the limits of safety before they begin to use them in the way you require. In some cases, this might be the first time they are seeing this material. Give them some time to become familiar with the material. Students are inquisitive. You need to factor into your lesson planning some familiarity time as part of your activity. If you rush into your planned procedures too quickly, you might stifle some potential learning and question asking. This initial familiarity with materials can lead to student questions you can use to develop your teaching activities.

7. **Establishing rules.** Try to anticipate any misuse of materials and the effects of overstimulation. If your students have had very few opportunities to interact with science materials in a classroom, their excitement over even seemingly mundane objects can be astonishing. Students who have never seen winged or multicolored seeds, will need time to explore before you begin an activity involving planting seeds. It might be necessary to establish some behavioral guidelines before the materials are distributed.

8. **Cleanup procedure.** Develop and maintain thorough cleanup procedures. You'll be doing yourself an enormous favor and also helping the students develop a worthwhile habit. You might assign a rotating cleanup detail until the students voluntarily assume the responsibility. Label your storage containers so that the objects can be easily identified and inventoried.

9. **Sharing materials with other teachers.** If you have to share your materials with other teachers, work together to establish clear rules to ensure that materials are always returned to their designated places and replaced if necessary.

Curriculum Development

Teacher Activity: **Focus Questions**

1. In planning, consider the following questions:

   How do I begin to plan my schedule?

   _____

   _____

   _____

2. How can I use standards to create a compliant curriculum?

   _____

   _____

   _____

An important aspect of the question "How do I get there?" involves looking at what other teachers have done as they plan their journeys.

Ideas from Other Science Teachers

EXAMPLE OF A GRADES 3–5 SCHEDULE FOR AN URBAN SCHOOL

Third Grade

1. Matter
   - Collect samples of the precipitation in order to experiment with the difference in density between—for example, snow and rain.

2. The Sun, Earth, and Moon System
   - Keep moon journals, observing different stages of the moon, as well as hypothesizing why the moon changes the way it does.
   - Measure and record the outside air pressure and temperature.
   - Observe different sky conditions, patterns of precipitation, and storms.
   - Record and chart the times of sunrise and sunset over a several month period.

3. Plant and Animal Characteristics

- Plant a garden and observe plants' life cycle; explore the concepts of seed dispersal, fruits, and the functions and parts of plants.
- Study an animal such as the pigeon to look for specific adaptations for survival by keeping an observational chart and comparing it to other birds and animals found in the neighborhood. Through the observations, students can begin to learn the difference between learned traits and inherited and acquired characteristics.

Fourth Grade

1. Exploring the Temperate Deciduous Forests and Other Ecosystems

- Take a nature walk around the school to observe the surroundings, both living and nonliving. Students will record their observations in a notebook. Students will learn that an ecosystem is made up of living and nonliving elements.

2. Forces and Motion

- Adopt a local construction site. Students can observe excavation and construction with particular attention to forces, friction, gravity, and simple machines.
- Analyze the structure of local bridges.

Fifth Grade

1. Healthy Planet II: Water, Land, and Air

- Test the water quality of any local body of water.
- Observe for visible signs of pollution, either in water or in the air.
- Take a trip to the local waste management plant to see the process firsthand.
- Take a trip to the local recycling center. Students could begin their own recycling project in order to help the school environment.
- Study the air in the neighborhood by testing it and keeping data, which can later be used to make a graph.

Source: Example provided by Lindsay McPherson and Andrea Elias.

Developing Your Own Curriculum Plan

Whatever your role in science teaching, here are some questions to think about as you develop the phases of your plan for each lesson within your curriculum.

Phase 1. Selecting and setting up your lesson

- What are your goals for the lesson?
- What is it you want your students to know and understand about science as a result of the lesson?
- How will you build on your students' previous knowledge?
- What concepts and ideas do your students need to know in order to begin the task?
- What questions will you ask to help your students access their prior knowledge?
- What misconceptions might your students have?
- What are your expectations for your students?
- What resources will your students have to use?
- Will students work independently, in pairs, or in small groups?
- How will you arrange the class?
- How will you introduce the lesson?

Phase 2. Supporting students as they engage in the lesson

- What questions will you ask to focus their thinking?
- What questions will you ask to assess your students understanding of concepts?
- How will you encourage your students to share their thinking with their peers?
- How will you ensure that all your students remain engaged?
- What will you do if some students finish the activity and become bored or disruptive?

Phase 3. Sharing and discussing the activity

- How will you orchestrate the class discussion so that you accomplish your goals?
- What specific questions will you ask so that your students will make sense of the scientific concepts you are teaching?
- What will you do in the following classes that will build on this lesson?
- Refer to the list of topics generated in Teacher Activity: Your State Standards and Teaching Topics on page 94 and brainstorm strategies for teaching those topics.

How Will You Know When You Have Arrived at Your Best Level of Practice?

There is no definite answer to this question. You never really arrive. You are always trying to be an effective science teacher and so you never completely arrive. You are always changing, your students are constantly changing, and the body of scientific knowledge is constantly changing. The state and national tests will tell you how your students are performing, but you want to do more than have your students perform well on standardized tests. You want them to be emerging scientists on their way to becoming scientifically literate. Tests are important, but it is important to look at additional feedback on your success in teaching science, which enables your students to emerge as scientists. The most appropriate way to answer this question is to closely examine what is happening to you and what is happening to your students as a result of their exposure to science.

At the end of each science class, reflect on the following questions:

- What went well today?
- How successful was my class?
- Why was it a success?
- What did not go well today?
- Where did I go wrong?
- What changes should I make in my class tomorrow?
- If I could repeat this lesson, what would I do differently?

By continuing to reflect on these questions after each class session, you will eventually discover your strengths and weaknesses. Use these reflections for honest self-confrontation and accurate self-evaluation and to plan for your day-to-day science teaching.

You will know that your students are being provided with adequate opportunities for learning science, according to the science professional development community and the U.S. DoE, if they are

- handling materials, living and nonliving, without fear
- designing, making, or manipulating apparatus using a variety of materials, including state-of-the-art technology and readily available items
- moving around freely and finding the materials they need
- discussing their work with each other or with you and classroom visitors
- busy doing things they feel are important

- trying to work out for themselves what to do from step to step
- not expecting to be told what to do
- puzzling over a problem
- comparing their ideas or observations with those of others

You will know that you have created a situation in which science can be learned if your students

- have a clear idea of what they want to find out, investigate, or observe
- take the initiative in suggesting what to do and how to set about it
- try out ideas "to see what happens"
- observe things closely by watching, listening, touching, smelling
- try different ways of approaching a problem
- classify things according to their properties or characteristics
- make some record of what they find out or observe
- use instruments for aiding observation or measurement
- devise and apply tests to find out what things will do
- make predictions of what they expect to find or to happen
- look for evidence to support the statements they make
- try to quantify their observations
- confirm their findings carefully before accepting them as evidence

If you are a success at teaching science, visitors to your classroom and school should easily be able to find answers to the following questions that you should also consider as you plan for teaching science. The answers will help you determine if you have arrived and will let visitors determine if real science is happening in your classroom and school.

Classroom

- Do you see displays related to science? Is there a science learning center?
- Are science-related drawings on the bulletin boards? Are there plants, terrariums, aquariums, or collections (of rocks or insects, etc.)?
- Do you see any science equipment in evidence? Are there magnifiers? Magnets? Pictures? Computers?
- In science classes, do students work with materials, or is the teacher always reading or demonstrating?
- Do students discuss their ideas, predictions, and explanations with each other as well as with the teacher?
- What facilities and resources are available to teach science?

- Does the teacher have clear goals and objectives for teaching science?

- How often is science taught? Every day, once a week, or infrequently?

- Are students given opportunities to do hands-on science projects?

- Are activities available for parents to use at home to supplement what is done at school?

- Are students taken on field trips?

- Do teachers welcome assistance from parents and community members?

School

- Does the school library contain science books? If so, are students encouraged to read them?

- Is there enough space in the classrooms or elsewhere in the school for students to conduct experiments?

- If the school budget for science is inadequate, has the teacher tried to obtain resources from private or public funding sources?

- Is there a family science night?

So now we are about to start leading your students on a journey of exploration into the world of science. You have been preparing for your journey of teaching budding scientists. You have collected all your gear—content, pedagogical strategies, standards, materials, and information on your fellow travelers. And now it is time to begin the journey.

Take-Away Thought

An effective science teacher has a well-structured but flexible plan. Time to walk the talk. Enjoy the journey.

Appendix 1

The National Science Education Standards and the Benchmarks for Science Literacy

What Are the *National Science Education Standards* for Grades 3–5?

The national and state standards provide the context in which you will be teaching science. In 1989, the National Governors Association endorsed national education goals and set the stage for the development of national education standards. The mathematics standards developed by the National Council of Teachers of Mathematics (NCTM) were the first national standards to appear. In 1991, the National Research Council (NRC) began the development of the *National Science Education Standards (NSES),* with support from the Department of Education and the National Science Foundation. In 1996, after input from numerous scientists, science educators, teachers, and other citizens, the final version was published. The objective of the *National Science Education Standards* is to help achieve scientific literacy for all members of our society. The NRC defines scientific literacy as the knowledge and understanding of scientific concepts and processes required for personal decision making, participation in civic and cultural affairs, and economic productivity. It also includes specific types of abilities.

The *National Science Education Standards* identify

- what it means to be a scientifically literate citizen
- what should be taught at various grade levels
- what knowledge and skills teachers should have
- how students should be assessed
- how school districts should implement curriculum changes that will result in greater scientific literacy

The *National Science Education Standards* (National Research Council, 1996, p. 22) include:

- **Standards for science teaching.** The science teaching standards describe what teachers of science at all grade levels should know and be able to do.

- **Standards for professional development for teachers of science.** The professional development standards present a vision for the development of professional knowledge and skill among teachers (http://www.nap.edu/ readingroom/books/nses/4.html).

- **Standards for assessment in science education.** The assessment standards provide criteria against which to judge the quality of assessment practices.

- **Standards for science content.** The science content standards outline what students should know, understand, and be able to do in the natural sciences over the course of K–12 education.

- **Standards for science education programs.** The science education program standards describe the conditions necessary for quality school science programs.

- **Standards for science education systems.** The science education system standards consist of criteria for judging the performance of the overall science education system.

The *National Science Education Standards* are standards for all Americans. Equity is an underlying principle for the *Standards* and should pervade all aspects of science education. They apply to all students, regardless of age, gender, cultural or ethnic background, disabilities, aspirations, or interest and motivation in science. Different students will achieve understanding in different ways, and different students will achieve different degrees of depth and breadth of understanding depending on interest, ability, and context. But all students can develop the knowledge and skills described in the *Standards,* even as some students go well beyond these levels.

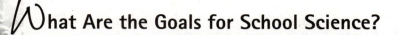

What Are the Goals for School Science?

The goals for school science that underlie the *National Science Education Standards* are to educate students who are able to:

- experience the richness and excitement of knowing about and understanding the natural world
- use appropriate scientific processes and principles in making personal decisions
- engage intelligently in public discourse and debate about matters of scientific and technological concern
- increase their economic productivity through the use of the knowledge, understanding, and skills developed in their science education

This section focuses only on the *Standards* for science content. You should, however, become familiar with standards for the other areas. The content standards, organized by K–4, 5–8, and 9–12 grade levels, provide expectations for the development of student understanding and ability over the course of K–12 education. Content is defined to include

- inquiry
- the traditional subject areas of physical, life, and earth and space sciences
- connections between science and technology
- science in personal and social perspectives
- the history and nature of science

The content standards are supplemented with information on developing student understanding, and they include fundamental concepts that underlie each standard.

Teacher Activity: Mapping the National Standards

Create an online folder or a hard copy in a folder or binder. As you complete the activities below, either store in your folder or print out the relevant standards and create your own current reference guide. This will be invaluable as you begin developing your class's curriculum.

1. Locate the national standards at: http://www.nap.edu/readingroom/books/nses/overview.html#organization or http://www.nap.edu/readingroom/books/nses.

2. Find the standards for grades 3–5, then print and file them.

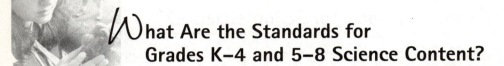

What Are the Standards for Grades K–4 and 5–8 Science Content?

Let us take a look at the standards for K–4 and 5–8 science content. This is the subdivision provided in the *NSES*.

The content standards do not dictate a national curriculum; however, they emphasize that the science experiences for grades K–12 need to be broad based. Each school and district must translate the *National Science Education Standards* into a program that reflects local contexts and policies. The program standards discuss the planning and actions needed to provide comprehensive and coordinated experiences for all students across all grade levels. The *Standards,* however, do not dictate the order, organization, or framework for science programs. Each state has the leeway to decide how programs will be enacted.

The instruction, program, and assessment that are emphasized by the *NSES* all promote the notion of inquiry in science teaching. What does inquiry mean in the context of science teaching? According to the *Standards,* inquiry into authentic questions generated from student experiences is the central strategy for teaching science. The *Standards* encourage teachers to focus on inquiry as it relates to the real-life experiences of students and to guide students to fashion their own investigations. Much of the current research in science education seeks to define what inquiry is, how it is enacted in the classroom, and how teachers can develop and implement inquiry-based experiences in their classrooms. As you begin to plan your science experiences for grades 3–5 students, you will realize that the term *inquiry* is used to describe a wide array of teaching strategies including discovery learning, learning-cycle-structured activities, open inquiry, and project-based learning. In general, the more direct experiences students have with materials, the greater the opportunity for them to ask and answer their own questions, thus leading to a deeper and more profound construction of their own understanding.

Teacher Activity: Standards Tables

As you begin to plan for teaching, complete Tables A1.1 and A1.2. The standard is listed in column 1; the content understanding that your 3–5 students need to develop in column 2. In column 3, you can list the inquiry and process skills that have been mentioned in association with this standard. Next, begin looking for Websites, textbooks, journals (e.g., *Science and Children*, an NSTA publication) for activities that you can use as you begin to plan for teaching and list these in column 4.

$\mathcal{T}$able A1.1   Standards for Grades K–4 Science Content

Standard	Content	Inquiry/Process Skills	Web/Text Reference for Activity
A	All students should develop • abilities necessary to do scientific inquiry • understanding about scientific inquiry		
B	All students should develop an understanding of • properties of objects and materials • position and motion of objects • light, heat, electricity, and magnetism		
C	All students should develop understanding of • characteristics of organisms • life cycles of organisms • organisms and environments		
D	All students should develop an understanding of • properties of earth materials • objects in the sky • changes in earth and sky		
E	All students should develop • abilities of technological design • understanding about science and technology • abilities to distinguish between natural objects and objects made by humans		

(continued on next page)

Table A1.1 Standards for Grades K–4 Science Content (continued)

Standard	Content	Inquiry/Process Skills	Web/Text Reference for Activity
F	All students should develop understanding of • personal health • characteristics and changes in populations • types of resources • changes in environments • science and technology in local challenges		
G	All students should develop understanding of • science as a human endeavor		

Table A1.2 Standards for Grades 5–8 Science Content

Standard	Content	Inquiry/Process Skills	Web/Text Reference for Activity
A	All students should develop • abilities necessary to do scientific inquiry • understandings about scientific inquiry		
B	All students should develop an understanding of • properties and changes of properties in matter • motions and forces • transfer of energy		
C	All students should develop understanding of • structure and function in living systems • reproduction and heredity • regulation and behavior • populations and ecosystems • diversity and adaptations of organisms		
D	All students should develop an understanding of • structure of the earth system • Earth's history • Earth in the solar system		
E	All students should develop • abilities of technological design • understanding about science and technology		

(continued on next page)

Table A1.2 Standards for Grades 5–8 Science Content (continued)

Standard	Content	Inquiry/Process Skills	Web/Text Reference for Activity
F	All students should develop understanding of • personal health • populations, resources, and environments • natural hazards • risks and benefits • science and technology in society		
G	All students should develop understanding of • science as a human endeavor • nature of science • history of science		

What Are the *Benchmarks for Science Literacy*?

The *Benchmarks for Science Literacy,* developed by Project 2061, specify how students should progress toward science literacy and recommend what they should know and be able to do by the time they reach certain grade levels. Project 2061's *Benchmarks* are statements of what all students should know or be able to do in science, mathematics, and technology by the end of grades 2, 5, 8, and 12. Table A1.3 lists these *Benchmarks*.

Teacher Activity: Using the *Benchmarks*

Table A1.3 lists the *Benchmarks* in columns 1 and 2. Fill in where the *Benchmark* is covered in your curriculum in column 3.

$\mathcal{T}$able A1.3   *Benchmarks for Science Literacy* for Grades 3–5

	What students should know by the end of the fifth grade	Where this is covered in my curriculum
The Scientific Worldview	• Sometimes similar investigations give different results because of differences in the things being investigated, the methods used, or the circumstances in which the investigation is carried out, and sometimes just because of uncertainties in observations. It is not always easy to tell which. • Science is a process of trying to figure out how the world works by making careful observations and trying to make sense of those observations.	
Scientific Inquiry	• Scientific investigations may take many different forms, including observing what things are like or what is happening somewhere, collecting specimens for analysis, and doing experiments. • Because we expect science investigations that are done the same way to produce the same results; when they do not, it is important to try to figure out why. • One reason for following directions carefully and for keeping records of one's work is to provide information on what might have caused differences in investigations. • Scientists' explanations about what happens in the world come partly from what they observe, partly from what they think. • Sometimes scientists have different explanations for the same set of observations. That usually leads to their making more observations to resolve the differences. • Scientists do not pay much attention to claims about how something they know about works unless the claims are backed up with evidence that can be confirmed, along with a logical argument.	

(continued on next page)

Table A1.3 *Benchmarks for Science Literacy* for Grades 3–5

	What students should know by the end of the fifth grade	Where this is covered in my curriculum
The Scientific Enterprise	• Science is an adventure that people everywhere can take part in, as they have for many centuries. • Clear communication is an essential part of doing science. It enables scientists to inform others about their work, expose their ideas to criticism by other scientists, and stay informed about scientific discoveries around the world. • Doing science involves many different kinds of work and engages men and women of all ages and backgrounds. • Many social practices and products of technology are shaped by scientific knowledge.	
Technology and Science	• Throughout all of history, people everywhere have invented and used tools. Most tools of today are different from those of the past but many are modifications of very ancient tools. • Technology enables scientists and others to observe things that are too small or too far away to be seen otherwise and to study the motion of objects that are moving very rapidly or are hardly moving at all. • Measuring instruments can be used to gather accurate information for making scientific comparisons of objects and events and for designing and constructing things that will work properly. • Technology extends the ability of people to change the world: to cut, shape, or put together materials; to move things from one place to another; and to reach further with their hands, voices, senses, and minds. The changes may be for survival needs (such as food, shelter, and defense), for communication and transportation, or to gain knowledge and express ideas.	

Table A1.3   *Benchmarks for Science Literacy* for Grades 3–5

	What students should know by the end of the fifth grade	Where this is covered in my curriculum
Design and Systems	• There is no perfect design. Designs that are best in one respect (safety or ease of use, for example) may be inferior in other ways (cost or appearance). Usually some features must be sacrificed to get others. • Even a good design may fail. Sometimes steps can be taken ahead of time to reduce the likelihood of failure, but it cannot be entirely eliminated. • The solution to one problem may create other problems.	
Issues in Technology	• Technology has been part of life on the earth since the advent of the human species. • Like language, ritual, commerce, and the arts, technology is an intrinsic part of human culture, and it both shapes society and is shaped by it. • The technology available to people greatly influences what their lives are like. • Any invention is likely to lead to other inventions. Once an invention exists, people are likely to think up ways of using it that were never imagined at first. • Transportation, communications, nutrition, sanitation, health care, entertainment, and other technologies give large numbers of people today the goods and services that once were luxuries enjoyed only by the wealthy. These benefits are not equally available to everyone. • Factors such as cost, safety, appearance, environmental impact, and what will happen if the solution fails must be considered in technological design. • Technologies often have drawbacks as well as benefits. A technology that helps some people or organisms may hurt others—either deliberately (as weapons can) or inadvertently (as pesticides can). • Because of their ability to invent tools and processes, people have an enormous effect on the lives of other living things.	

(continued on next page)

Table A1.3 *Benchmarks for Science Literacy* for Grades 3–5

	What students should know by the end of the fifth grade	Where this is covered in my curriculum
The Universe	• The patterns of stars in the sky stay the same, although they appear to move across the sky nightly, and different stars can be seen in different seasons. • Telescopes magnify the appearance of some distant objects in the sky, including the moon and the planets. The number of stars that can be seen through telescopes is dramatically greater than can be seen by the unaided eye. • Planets change their positions against the background of stars. • The Earth is one of several planets that orbit the sun, and the moon orbits around the Earth. • Stars are like the sun, some being smaller and some larger, but so far away that they look like points of light. • A large light source at a great distance looks like a small light source that is much closer.	

$Table A1.3$ *Benchmarks for Science Literacy* for Grades 3–5

	What students should know by the end of the fifth grade	Where this is covered in my curriculum
The Earth	• Things on or near the Earth are pulled toward it by the Earth's gravity. • The Earth is approximately spherical in shape. Like the Earth, the sun and planets are spheres. • The rotation of the Earth on its axis every twenty-four hours produces the night-and-day cycle. To people on Earth, this turning of the planet makes it seem as though the sun, moon, planets, and stars are orbiting the Earth once a day. • When liquid water disappears, it turns into a gas (vapor) in the air and can reappear as a liquid when cooled, or as a solid if cooled below the freezing point of water. Clouds and fog are made of tiny droplets or frozen crystals of water. • Air is a material that surrounds us and takes up space and whose movement we feel as wind. • The weather is always changing and can be described by measurable quantities such as temperature, wind direction and speed, and precipitation. Large masses of air with certain properties move across the surface of the Earth. The movement and interaction of these air masses is used to forecast the weather.	
Processes that Shape the Earth	• Waves, wind, water, and ice shape and reshape the Earth's land surface by eroding rock and soil in some areas and depositing them in other areas, sometimes in seasonal layers. • Rock is composed of different combinations of minerals. Smaller rocks come from the breakage and weathering of bedrock and larger rocks. Soil is made partly from weathered rock, partly from plant remains—and also contains many living organisms.	

(continued on next page)

Table A1.3   *Benchmarks for Science Literacy* for Grades 3–5

	What students should know by the end of the fifth grade	Where this is covered in my curriculum
The Structure of Matter	• Heating and cooling can cause changes in the properties of materials, but not all materials respond the same way to being heated and cooled. • Many kinds of changes occur faster under hotter conditions. • No matter how parts of an object are assembled, the weight of the whole object is always the same as the sum of the parts; and when an object is broken into parts, the parts have the same total weight as the original object. • Materials may be composed of parts that are too small to be seen without magnification. • When a new material is made by combining two or more materials, it has properties that are different from the original materials. • A lot of different materials can be made from a small number of basic kinds of materials. • All materials have certain physical properties, such as strength, hardness, flexibility, durability, resistance to water and fire, and ease of conducting heat. • Collections of pieces (powders, marbles, sugar cubes, or wooden blocks) may have properties that the individual pieces do not. • Substances may move from place to place, but they never appear out of nowhere and never just disappear.	
Energy Transformations	• When two objects are rubbed against each other, they both get warmer. In addition, many mechanical and electrical devices get warmer when they are used. • When warmer things are put with cooler ones, the warmer things get cooler and the cooler things get warmer until they all are the same temperature. • When warmer things are put with cooler ones, heat is transferred from the warmer ones to the cooler ones. • A warmer object can warm a cooler one by contact or at a distance.	

Table A1.3   *Benchmarks for Science Literacy* for Grades 3–5

	What students should know by the end of the fifth grade	Where this is covered in my curriculum
Motion	• Changes in speed or direction of motion are caused by forces. • The greater the force is, the greater the change in motion will be. The more massive an object is, the less effect a given force will have. • How fast things move differs greatly. Some things are so slow that their journey takes a long time; others move too fast for people to even see them. • Light travels and tends to maintain its direction of motion until it interacts with an object or material. Light can be absorbed, redirected, bounced back, or allowed to pass through.	
Forces of Nature	• The Earth's gravity pulls any object on or near the Earth toward it without touching it. • Without touching them, a magnet pulls on all things made of iron and either pushes or pulls on other magnets. • Without touching them, an object that has been electrically charged pulls on all other uncharged objects and may either push or pull other charged objects.	
Diversity of Life	• A great variety of kinds of living things can be sorted into groups in many ways using various features to decide which things belong to which group. • There are millions of different kinds of individual organisms that inhabit the earth at any one time—some very similar to each other, some very different.	
Hereditary	• Some likenesses between children and parents are inherited. Other likenesses are learned. • For offspring to resemble their parents, there must be a reliable way to transfer information from one generation to the next.	

(continued on next page)

Table A1.3 *Benchmarks for Science Literacy* for Grades 3–5

	What students should know by the end of the fifth grade	Where this is covered in my curriculum
Cells	• Some living things consist of a single cell. Like familiar organisms, they need food, water, and air; a way to dispose of waste; and an environment they can live in. • Microscopes make it possible to see that living things are made mostly of cells. • Some organisms are made of a collection of similar cells that benefit from cooperating. Some organisms' cells vary greatly in appearance and perform very different roles in the organism.	
Interdependence of Life	• For any particular environment, some kinds of plants and animals thrive, some do not live as well, and some do not survive at all. • Insects and various other organisms depend on dead plant and animal material for food. • Organisms interact with one another in various ways besides providing food. • Many plants depend on animals for carrying their pollen to other plants or for dispersing their seeds. • Changes in an organism's habitat are sometimes beneficial to it and sometimes harmful. • Most microorganisms do not cause disease, and many are beneficial	
Flow of Matter and Energy	• Almost all kinds of animals' food can be traced back to plants. • Some source of "energy" is needed for all organisms to stay alive and grow. • Over the Earth, organisms are growing, dying, decaying, and new organisms are being produced by the old ones.	
Evolution of Life	• Individuals of the same kind differ in their characteristics, and sometimes the differences give individuals an advantage in surviving and reproducing. • Fossils can be compared to one another and to living organisms according to their similarities and differences. Some organisms that lived long ago are similar to existing organisms, but some are quite different.	

Appendix *2*

Science Content Information for Grades 3–5

Third Grade

Plant and Animal Adaptations

In order to teach the content of plant and animal adaptations, teachers should know:

1. All living things grow through taking in nutrients and using these nutrients to grow, reproduce, and eliminate waste.

- Different organisms perform these functions differently. For example, humans use their mouths for eating as well as breathing but excrete wastes through a separate anus and urethra. Certain worm species eat and eliminate waste through the same opening. Plants rely on their roots to take in nutrients to grow leaves and flowers that animals then eat as nutrients for their own growth.

- Plants adapt to their environment in order to survive.

- Form and function are related.
  - Leaves of certain desert plants have a very waxy cuticle on their leaves to keep water from evaporating. Weeping willow trees have very long roots that reach into the river banks. Mangrove trees which can live in areas with lots of salt and water, prop themselves up above the water level with stilt roots, and can then take in air through pores in their bark.
- Biological structures can vary in size, shape, thickness, color, smell, and texture.
- Plants change with the seasons (for example, the leaves of some plants can wilt and fall off until they bloom again in the summer).
- Dispersion of seeds through many different mechanisms can improve their chances of survival.

2. Animals, like plants, also increase their chances of survival through adaptation.
   - Structure and function is important.
     - Wings, legs, fins, scales, feathers, and fur are all features that have adapted, over time, and help animals survive and thrive in their environment.
   - Animals can also respond immediately to changes in the environment. These are physiological changes while the changes discussed above are structural and have evolved. Physiological changes are immediate.
     - Heart rate increases when an animal is scared or running.
     - Eyes blink in response to changes in quality of air to protect the eye or in response to changes in light. Eyes blink less when fixated on prey.
     - Animals shiver in response to being cold to raise their body temperature.
   - Animals can also adapt to changes in seasons.
     - Some animals hibernate in response to a scarcity of food when winter comes, such as bears.
     - Some animals migrate to meet their needs. Certain birds fly south for the winter, as do some people.

3. Traits of living things can be both inherited (passed on through genes from generation to generation) or acquired and learned (traits that evolve as a result of one's experiences interacting in the world).
   - Inherited traits include the color of a flower or the color of eyes.
   - Acquired and learned traits could include an ability to drive a car.

Matter

In order to teach the content of matter, teachers should know:

1. The physical properties of objects can be measured using standard (metric) and nonstandard units (e.g., a hand).

   - Comparisons of physical properties of objects can be described using appropriate tools such as rulers, thermometers, pan balances, spring scales, graduated cylinders and beakers.

2. Matter can be described based on its physical properties, using words such as size, shape, mass or weight, volume, flexibility, luster, texture, hardness, and odor.

Texas state standards require that students identify the states of matter.

Energy

In order to teach the content of energy, teachers should know:

1. Energy can be transmitted in many different ways: sound, heat, light, mechanical, electrical, and chemical.

2. Energy can be transmitted or transformed by chemical and physical reactions.

3. Energy can be transformed from one form to another and is involved in all biological activities—energy transformation is going on in our bodies all day, every day!

   - Heat energy can be transformed to light.

   - Chemical energy can be transformed to electrical energy.

   - Electrical energy can be transformed to sound.

4. Heat is able to be conducted and can be transferred from one place to another.

   - An ice cube is placed in a glass of warm water. The ice cube melts as heat is transferred from the water to the ice.

   - Heat can be released in a number of ways, including, through burning, rubbing, or combining one substance with another (i.e., warm water and ice cube).

5. Matter and energy interact with each other.

   - Electricity lights a bulb, and the dark colors of a T-shirt absorb heat energy (solar energy) from the light.

6. Sound has distinct characteristics that can be described in terms of pitch or frequency, amplitude, vibrations, and volume.

- Sound travels differently through different substances: solids, liquids and gases

  - Sound travels fastest through solids because the particles in a solid are tightly packed and touching. A sound wave touching one particle almost immediately transfers the energy to its neighbor.

  - Sound travels second fastest through liquids, because the particles of liquids are closer together than that of a gas but farther apart than those of a solid.

  - Sound travels the slowest and least efficiently through gases, because the particles are so spread out.

- Sound needs a medium to travel through; sound cannot be transferred in a vacuum.

- Noise pollution can be caused by many sources, including highways, vehicles, factories, concerts, air conditioners, engines, machines, aircraft, and alarms.

California state standards review the three states of matter: solid, liquid, and gas.

- Evaporation and melting are changes that occur when substances are heated.

- All matter is made up of small particles (atoms), which are too small to be seen with the naked eye.

- Light has a source and travels in a direction.

Simple Machines

In order to teach the content of plant diversity, teachers should know:

1. The application of force or the use of simple machines may cause motion through the use of mechanical energy.

2. Simple machines include levers, pulleys, inclined planes, wheels and axels, wedges, and screws.

3. Friction can result in a force that impedes motion.

4. The position and motion of an object can be changed by pushing or pulling (applying a force).

5. Gravity is a force that acts on all objects, pulling them toward the center of the Earth.

- When a ball is thrown, it does not continue traveling forever, because the force of gravity is pulling it back down to the Earth and because of friction from the atmosphere.

Earth Science

In order to teach the content of earth science, teachers should know:

1. The natural world includes both materials in the earth and in the sky.
   - Rocks, soil, water, and gases of the atmosphere can be classified as renewable, nonrenewable, or inexhaustible, based on their availability.
     - Nonrenewable resources exist in a fixed amount or are used up faster than they can be replaced by nature (i.e., fossil fuels, such as coal).
     - Renewable resources are natural resources that can be used more than once (i.e., oxygen, fresh water, and solar energy).
     - Inexhaustible resources exist in such large supply that they can be considered almost limitless (e.g., rocks).

2. There are eight planets, including Earth, in our solar system
   - They all orbit the sun.
   - The moon orbits Earth.

3. The sun is a star in the center of our solar system composed of gases, including helium and hydrogen. The sun produces energy internally, which is transmitted externally to its planets in the form of sunlight. On Earth, this drives photosynthesis in plants and provides the temperature that supports life on Earth. It influences the climate of Earth.
   - The position of the sun in the sky changes during the day as the Earth rotates (24 hours = 1 rotation). The rotation of Earth results in variations in light we call day and night. The revolution of Earth around the sun (1 revolution = 365 days) in combination with the 23.5 degree tilt of Earth on its axis causes the seasons.

4. The moon changes appearance over time. The changes of the moon are cyclical and have phases.
   - The phases of the moon that we see result from the angle the moon makes with the sun as we view it from Earth.
     - The waxing periods when the moon appears to be getting larger are: new, crescent, first quarter, gibbous.
     - The waning periods when the moon appears to be getting smaller are: full, gibbous, third quarter, crescent.

Texas and California both emphasize earth science in third grade.

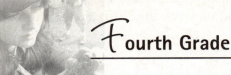

Fourth Grade

Animals and Plants

In order to teach the content of plants and animals, teachers should know:

1. Communities of organisms make up ecosystems (food chains and food webs). Within the ecosystem there are producers, consumers (herbivores, omnivores, carnivores), and decomposers.

    ● Producers—organisms that make their own organic material (food). They form the basis of the food web. Plants produce food by photosynthesis and other chemical processes for consumers (animals and humans).

    ● Consumers—organisms within a biological community that cannot manufacture their own food and therefore depend on other organisms for their nutritional supply. All consumers (animals and humans) rely on producers (like plants and other animals) for food.

    ● Decomposers—organisms such as bacteria, fungi, earthworms, and vultures that feed on dead animals and plants, as well as other organic wastes, and break them down physically and chemically, thus supplying food for others in the food web.

    ● Ecosystem—a system consisting of a community of animals, plants, and microorganisms, abiotic factors, and the physical and chemical environment in which they interrelate.

2. Plants manufacture some of their own food by utilizing air, water, and energy from the sun in a process called photosynthesis.

3. Food supplies energy and materials necessary for growth and repair to living things.

4. Within a population, resources can be limited. Individual populations within a community can compete with one another for the same resources.

5. Within a species, individual variations can develop that can provide an advantage in surviving and reproducing.

6. The color of an individual animal's coat may help it better hide from predators by blending in better with the environment. Another individual within a species may be stronger and able to fight off the competition for mating rights (such as the alpha male in a lion pride).

7. The health, growth, and development of organisms are affected by environmental conditions. The availability of water, food, air, space, shelter,

heat, and sunlight all are important factors in determining the well-being of an organism and will affect their ability to thrive.

8. Animals use their senses in order to survive.

   - Dogs have an excellent sense of smell and use this sense to find food or to smell the presence of other animals. (This adept sense of smell is one of the reasons why dogs are used in law enforcement.)

   - Snakes, some lizards, and cats can smell with their tongues. (Lizards have what is called a Jacobson's organ on the roof of their mouths. When the tongue is brought back in the mouth, it is placed on the Jacobson's organ, causing a physical reaction that is interpreted by the brain.)

   - The forked tongue of snakes and some lizards helps them pick up scent molecules to find the direction of a scent.

   - Some invertebrates, like butterflies, taste with different sense organs, which are located on their feet.

9. When environmental changes occur, some plants and animals survive and reproduce, while others die or move to new locations.

   - Dinosaurs and other prehistoric organisms thrived in the Jurassic period. However, when conditions on Earth changed, some became extinct. Some species of fish, however, were able to survive the climate change and continued to reproduce.

10. Humans depend on their natural and constructed environment and have changed that environment over time in order to better meet their needs.

    - Human activity can have both beneficial and harmful effects on other organisms. For example, deforestation in the Amazon has eliminated certain species and put others on the endangered species list.

Electricity and Magnetism

In order to teach the content of electricity and magnetism, teachers should know:

1. Electrical energy can be transferred in electrical circuits.

   - Circuits are the path along which an electrical current flows.

2. Simple circuits require

   - a source of electrical potential difference or voltage (typically a battery or electrical outlet)

   - a conductive path that will allow for the movement of charges (in domestic applications, typically made of wire)

- an electrical resistance (resistor), which can be something that uses electricity to do work (a lightbulb, electric motor, heating element, speaker, etc.)

3. Open circuits—a circuit having some break in it so that current is not passing or cannot pass.

4. Closed circuits—a circuit having a complete path for current flow.

5. Switches—a device that opens or closes circuits or selects the path of circuits to be used.

6. Conductors and insulators can be part of an electric circuit.

- Conductors are materials that permit electricity to flow. Typically, conductors are metallic. In home building, contractors use copper, aluminum, and copper-coated aluminum.

- Insulators are materials that prevent the flow of heat (thermal insulators) or electric charge (electrical insulators). Electric insulators are typically made of glass or porcelain and are used to support electrical wires to prevent the unwanted flow of electricity.

7. Different materials have varying magnetic and electrical properties.

8. Magnets attract and repel certain objects.

- Magnets can attract or repel each other.

- Magnetic forces can operate on objects across distances and through materials (i.e., two magnets can move each other when one is on top of the table and the other is underneath the table).

- Magnets produce a magnetic field.

9. Electricity and magnetism can interact to create an electromagnet.

- Electromagnet—a coil of wire wound about a magnetic material, such as iron, that produces a magnetic field when current flows through the wire.

10. Electricity can be both helpful and harmful to people.

- Electricity is helpful in that it provides the energy to turn on lights and to cook food or run a hair dryer. However electricity can be harmful to people in that it can send a shock to the body that can result in death.

Properties of Water

In order to teach about the properties of water, teachers should know:

1. Water can exhibit different physical properties depending on its temperature and what is dissolved in it.

- Water at temperatures supporting human habitation is a liquid.
- Water changes its shape to fit the space occupied by its container.
- The mass and volume of liquid water can change a little with temperature.

2. Different factors affect evaporation. Liquid and gas molecules are always moving. At the water's surface, some molecules are bumped by molecules below them and gain enough speed to break free and escape into the air as gas (water vapor). This escape of surface molecules involves a change of state from liquid to gas.

- Temperature—The higher the temperature, the higher the rate of evaporation. When the temperature of water is increased, the water molecules gain more energy, move faster, and escape at a higher rate.
- Exposed surface area—With a larger exposed area, more heat and wind can come into contact with the water molecules at any one time. Therefore, the rate of evaporation is higher. This is why when your clothes get wet, you should spread them out to dry rather than leaving them in a ball.
- Wind—When evaporation takes place, the water vapor gathers above the water's surface. When there is wind, the water vapor is removed as soon as it is formed. This makes space for more water molecules to escape into the air. The stronger the wind, the higher the rate of evaporation.
- Humidity—If water evaporates in a closed container, the space above the water is filled with more and more water vapor. When the air contains a lot of water vapor, humidity is high. When humidity is high, it is more difficult for water to evaporate.

3. The water cycle (also known as the hydrologic cycle) is the journey water takes as it circulates from the land to the sky and back again.

- The sun's heat provides energy to evaporate water from Earth's surface (oceans, lakes, etc.). Plants also lose water to the air (this is called transpiration). The water vapor eventually condenses, forming tiny droplets in clouds. When the clouds meet cool air over land, precipitation (rain, sleet, or snow) is triggered, and water returns to the land (or sea). Some of the precipitation soaks into the ground. Some of the underground water is trapped between rock or clay layers; this is called groundwater. But most of the water flows downhill as runoff (above ground or underground), eventually returning to the seas as slightly salty water.

4. Different objects sink and float depending on their material, density, and shape.

5. Different substances have differing abilities to mix with water.

   • Oil is a slippery or viscous material that cannot be dissolved in water.

   • Sugar is a white crystalline carbohydrate, used as a sweetener and pre-servative, that can be dissolved in water. Substances must be soluble in water to mix thoroughly with it.

6. Matter can be transformed from one form to another.

   • Solid water in the form of ice can be melted to form a liquid. Liquid water can be heated to evaporate in the form of a gas (water vapor). A gas can be condensed to form a liquid when cooled. Liquid can then be cooled to form a solid (ice).

   • Condensation—the process in which water vapor changes into liquid water.

   • Evaporation—Water molecules are always moving. At the water's surface, some molecules are bumped by molecules below them and gain enough speed to break free and escape into the air as gas (water vapor). This escape of surface molecules involves a change of state from liquid to gas.

7. The sun is the major source of heat energy.

   • The addition and reduction of heat is a common cause of changes in states of matter (temperature, melting, and evaporation).

8. Materials can undergo physical changes.

   Physical changes in materials can include change in size, form, shape, and temperature.

Interactions of Air, Water, and Land

In order to teach about the interactions of air, water and land, teachers should know:

1. Weathering can include chemical and physical change.

   • Physical weathering (mechanical weathering)—the breakdown of rocks and soils through direct contact with atmospheric conditions such as wind, heat, water, ice, and pressure.

   Causes

   ■ Thermal expansion—When a rock heats up during the day and cools quickly at night (like in deserts), stress occurs and the outer surface of the rock begins to peel off.

   ■ Frost-induced weathering

   ■ Pressure

   ■ Hydraulic action—Water, generally from big waves, rushes into the cracks of a rock's surface. When the wave retreats, air is left in the spaces between the rocks and builds up pressure, causing the rock to crack even further when the air is released in an explosive force.

- Chemical weathering—the direct effect of atmospheric chemicals, or biologically produced chemicals, in the breakdown of rocks, soils, and minerals.

  Causes

  - Acid in acid rain can wear down rocks, soil, etc.

  - Atoms in water (H+, OH–) attach to the atoms and minerals of a rock, causing the rock to expand in size and subsequently become stressed a process called hydrolysis.

  - Oxidation—Occurs when metals, oxygen and water combine. The resulting hydroxides and oxides weaken the rocks and make them crumble.

  - Acidic compounds can be released by plants.

  - The materials left over from weathering, combined with organic material, create soil.

  - Events such as volcanic eruptions and earthquakes are responsible for Earth movements.

  - Models can be used to understand the different landforms.

2. Erosion through gravity, wind, and water cause surface changes to the land.

   - Erosion is the displacement of solids (soil, mud, rock, and other particles) by the agents of ocean currents, wind, water, or ice, by downward or down-slope movement in response to gravity or other pressures. A certain amount of erosion is natural and, in fact, healthy for the ecosystem. For example, gravel continuously moves downstream in watercourses. Excessive erosion, however, does cause problems, such as sedimentation, ecosystem damage, and outright loss of soil.

     - Human activities that unnaturally increase the rates of erosion include deforestation, unchecked building, and overgrazing.

     - Improved land uses, such as terraces for planting and planting trees, can limit human impact and erosion.

3. Water is recycled on Earth by natural processes.

4. Extreme natural events have both negative and positive impacts on living things.

   - Earthquakes—result from the sudden release of stored energy in the Earth's crust that creates seismic waves. At the Earth's surface, earthquakes may manifest themselves by a shaking or displacement of the ground. Sometimes, they cause tsunamis. An earthquake is caused by tectonic plates forcing each other to move. The pressure produced becomes so great that rocks give way by breaking and sliding along fault planes.

- Positive effects—Mountains are being created, minerals from below are being brought up, and new sea floors are being made.

- Negative effects—destruction of land, displacement of species.

- Volcanoes—an opening, or rupture, in the Earth's surface or crust that allows hot, molten rock and ash and gases to escape from deep below the surface. Volcanic activity involving the extrusion of rock tends to form mountains or features like mountains over a period of time. Volcanoes are generally found where tectonic plates are interacting.

- Positive effects

  - Provide nutrients to the surrounding soil. Volcanic ash often contains minerals that are beneficial to plants, and if it is very fine ash it is able to break down quickly and get mixed into the soil.

  - Volcanic slopes are often rather inaccessible, especially if they are steep. Thus, they can provide refuges for rare plants and animals from the ravages of humans and livestock.

  - Volcanic gases are the source of all the water (and most of the atmosphere) that we have today.

- Negative effects

  - Plants are destroyed over a wide area, during an eruption.

  - Aquatic life can be affected by an increase in acidity, increased turbidity, change in temperature, and/or change in food supply. These factors can damage or kill fish.

  - Bird migration can be affected.

  - Eruptions release sulfurs into the air, which can be carried by trade winds and effect the rain causing pollution, acid rain, etc.

- Other extreme events include hurricanes, tornadoes, floods, and fires.

Texas state standards also require students to know that certain past events affect present and future events. Some events—such as growing, erosion, dissolving, weathering, and flow—require time for change to be noticeable. Additionally, students should be able to draw conclusions about "what happened before," using fossils or charts and tables.

California state standards in their earth sciences units require students to understand the properties of rocks and minerals as well as the processes that formed them. Students should be able to differentiate between igneous, sedimentary, and metamorphic rocks by referring to their properties and methods of formation (rock cycle).

Fifth Grade

Earth Science

In order to teach the content of earth science, teachers should know:

1. Rocks and minerals are different.

   - Rock—a naturally occurring aggregate of minerals and/or mineraloids.

   - The Earth's lithosphere is made of rock.

   - In general rocks are of three types namely, igneous, sedimentary, and metamorphic.

   - Petrology—the scientific study of rocks.

   - Rocks are classified by mineral and chemical composition, by the texture of the particles they are made of and by the processes that formed them. These characteristics separate rocks into igneous, sedimentary, and metamorphic.

     - Rocks may also be classified according to particle size, in the case of conglomerates and breccias or in the case of individual stones. The transformation of one rock type to another is described by the geological model called the rock cycle.

   - Minerals—naturally occurring substances formed through geological processes.

     - Minerals have a characteristic chemical composition, a highly ordered atomic structure, and specific physical properties.

     - Minerals range in what they are made up of including from pure elements and simple salts to very complex silicates with thousands of known forms.

   - The study of minerals is called mineralogy.

2. Topographical maps, also called contour maps, are land maps that display elevation along with natural and man-made features.

   - Interpreting topographic maps

     - Thin brown lines represent contours or points of similar elevation. The closer together they are, the steeper the terrain.

     - Contour lines form "V" shapes in valleys or along stream beds. The point of the "V" points uphill.

     - Blue represents water.

     - Green represents orchards and forested areas.

- Purple markings are those that have been added to the map since the original map was published.

- Red areas represent urban areas, although the maps will often indicate special buildings of significance within the urbanized area.

- Roads and highways are represented in black and red.

3. Erosion is the process by which particles of rock and soil are loosened, transported, and deposited elsewhere by processes such as wind, water, ice, or gravity (rockslides and mudslides).

4. Deposition is the end product of erosion. During deposition, the loosened particles from erosion settle.

- Erosion is responsible for the creation of hills and valleys.

- Excessive erosion can be problematic. Man-made structures, such as houses along shorelines and coasts, can enhance the erosion process.

- Some controls for excess erosion include contour plowing, terrace farming, planting ground cover (roots holding the soil), building seawalls and sand dunes.

5. Weathering is the breakdown of rocks, soil, and minerals through their contact with the atmosphere, which includes water and wind.

In California, there is a focus on water sources, cycles, and renewable resources. Teachers should know that water on Earth moves between the oceans and land through the processes of evaporation and condensation. Additionally, most of Earth's surface is covered with salt water found in the oceans. When the water from the oceans and other land surfaces evaporates, it turns into water vapor in the air and can reappear as a liquid when cooled or as a solid if cooled below the freezing point of water. Water vapor in the air moves from one place to another and can form fog or clouds or fall as forms of precipitation (rain, hail, sleet, or snow). The amount of fresh water that is located in rivers, lakes, underground sources, and glaciers is limited. In order to maintain the stores of fresh water, certain initiatives can be taken to recycle the water, such as decreasing the use of fresh water in everyday activities and reverse osmosis technologies and other purification techniques. It is also important that students in California be able to know the origin of water used by their local communities.

In Texas, there is also an emphasis on renewable and nonrenewable resources as well as some additional topics relating to landforms and using data to understand what happened before. Teachers should know that by using data generated from tree growth rings and sedimentary rock sequences, you can draw conclusions as to when certain events occurred. Teachers should be familiar with the processes that are responsible for the formation of coal, oil, gas, and minerals. Additionally, comparisons should be made between the physical characteristics of the Earth and the moon.

Food and Nutrition

In order to teach the content of food and nutrition, teachers should know:

1. Humans need a variety of healthy foods, exercise, and rest in order to grow and maintain good health.

   - Healthy foods include a diet rich in fruits, vegetables, and protein as well as whole grains and limited amounts of fat.

   - Nutritionists and doctors suggest 60 minutes a day of exercise and on average 7.5 hours to 9 hours a week.

2. Good health habits include hand washing and personal cleanliness, avoiding harmful substances (including alcohol, tobacco, illicit drugs), eating a balanced diet, and engaging in regular exercise.

3. The health, growth, and development of organisms are affected by environmental conditions such as the availability of food, air, water, space, shelter, heat, and sunlight.

4. Food supplies the energy and materials necessary for growth and repair.

   - Food can be considered at the level of the cell, the system, and the organism. The digestive and the circulatory systems work together to distribute food components to the cells. Inside the cell, molecular reactions occur that enable reproduction and growth of the cells, which, in turn, enable the organism to grow and reproduce. Protein found in food is essential for protein synthesis within cells .

   - When food is consumed by an organism, it is broken down into smaller chemical components by both physical and chemical digestion for use by the body.

Ecosystems

In order to teach about ecosystems, teachers should know:

1. An ecosystem is a system consisting of a community of animals, plants, and microorganisms and the physical and chemical environments in which they interrelate.

   - The biodiversity of an ecosystem, including the biotic and abiotic factors, is what helps the ecosystem to thrive and remain resilient.

     - Water, temperature, plants, animals, air, light, and soil all work together. If there isn't enough light or water or if the soil doesn't have the right nutrients, the plants will die. If the plants die, animals that depend on them will die. If the animals that depend on the plants die, any animals that depend on those animals will die. All the parts work together to make a balanced system.

- There are different classifications of ecosystems, including marine/aquatic, desert, tropical rainforest, temperate forest, grassland, and tundra/taiga.

  - Forest ecosystems include everything from trees, shrubs, herbs, bacteria, and fungi to animals and people, together with the environmental substrate of the air, soil, water, organic debris, and rocks.

  - Forest ecosystems grow in a variety of climates and can be found in tropical forests, arctic mountain slopes, and various coastlines. The type of forest in a particular place is based on the climate, the patterns of rainfall, seed availability, soils, and factors such as human impact.

2. Plants use air, water, and energy from the sun to produce their own food.

- A key process of food making in plants is termed *photosynthesis*. During photosynthesis, carbon dioxide, light, and water are converted into oxygen and glucose using energy from the sun. The chemical process in which oxygen is used to make energy from carbohydrates is cellular respiration. The equation for photosynthesis is

$$6H_2O + 6CO_2 \rightarrow C_6H_{12}O_6 + 6O_2$$

The chemical equation translates as: six molecules of water plus six molecules of carbon dioxide produce one molecule of sugar plus six molecules of oxygen.

- Plants are considered autotrophs because they are able to make their own food. Other organisms depend on the energy stored in plants for their own survival. Animals are considered consumers because they eat plants in order to gain energy for their own needs.

3. Food supplies the energy and materials necessary for growth and repair of living organisms.

- Food can be considered at the level of the cell, the system, and the organism. The digestive and the circulatory systems work together to distribute food components to the cells. Inside the cell, chemical processes enable growth and multiplication of cells, which, in turn, enable the organism to grow and multiply. Protein, fat, sugar, and minerals ingested in food are essential to protein synthesis within cells.

- When food is digested by an organism, it is broken down into smaller chemical components for use by the body.

4. Depending on the role they serve in an ecosystem, populations can be classified as producers, consumers, or decomposers.

   - Food chains—the relationship between plants and animals that shows who eats what. Energy cycles from one organism to another through the food chain.

   - Food webs—a network of food chains.

5. Populations in a community can be in competition with one another for resources.

6. Humans depend on their natural and constructed environment for survival and have changed the environment over time to suit their needs.

   - At times human activity can have a harmful effect on other organisms; for example, deforestation, which displaces organisms.

   - Human activity, such as the preservation of space and the creation of sanctuaries, has had a beneficial effect in preserving certain organisms from extinction.

Physical Science

In order to teach the content of physical science content, teachers should know:

1. Elements and their combinations account for all the varied types of matter in the world.

   - During chemical reactions, the atoms in the reactants rearrange to form products with different properties.

   - All matter is made of atoms, which may combine to form molecules.

   - Metals have properties in common.

2. Elements are organized in the periodic table by their chemical properties.

References

Chapter 1

Gardner, H. (1991). *The unschooled mind: How children think and how schools should teach*. New York: Basic Books.

Gardner, H. (1993). *Creating minds: An anatomy of creativity*. New York: Basic Books.

Gardner, H. (1993). *Frames of mind: The theory of multiple intelligences*. New York: Basic Books.

Gardner, H. (1999). *The disciplined mind: Beyond facts and standardized tests, the K–12 education that every child deserves*. New York: Penguin Putnam.

Gardner, H. (1999). *Intelligence reframed: Multiple intelligences for the 21st century*. New York: Basic Books.

Gardner, H. (2005). *Development and education of mind: The selected works of Howard Gardner*. New York: Routledge.

Gardner, H. (2006). *Multiple intelligences: New horizons in theory and practice*. New York: Basic Books.

Gardner, H. (2007). *Five minds for the future*. Cambridge: Harvard Business School Press.

Koch, J. (2005). *Science stories: Science methods for elementary and middle school teachers*, 3rd ed. New York: Houghton Mifflin.

U.S. Department of Education, Office for Civil Rights, National Center for Education Statistics (NCES), Common Core of Data (CCD). *Public elementary/secondary school universe survey, 1991–92 to 2005–06*. Washington, DC: Author.

Chapter 2

Ahn, W., Gelman, S. A., Amsterlaw, J. A., Hohenstein, J., & Kalish, C. W. (2000). Causal status effects in children's categorization. *Cognition, 76*, 35–43.

Baillargeon, R. (2004). How do infants learn about the physical world? *Current Directions in Psychological Science, 3*, 133–140.

Bar, V., & Travis, A. S. (1991). Children's views concerning phase changes. *Journal of Research in Science Teaching, 28*(4), 363–382.

Barab, S. A., & Luehmann, A. L. (2002). Building a sustainable science curriculum: Acknowledging and accommodating local adaptation. *Journal of the Learning Sciences, 10*(4), 320–351.

Barker, M. (1995). A plant is an animal standing on its head. *Journal of Biological Education, 29*(3), 203–208.

Barman, C. R. (1997). Students' views of scientists and science: Results from a national study. *Science and Children, 35*(1), 18–24.

Barman, C. R. (1999). Students' views about scientists and school science: Engaging K–8 teachers in a national study. *Journal of Science Teacher Education, 10*(1), 43–54.

Barman, C., Barman, N., Cox, M. L., Newhouse, K., & Goldston, M. J. (2000). Students' ideas about animals: Results from a national study. *Science and Children, 38*(1), 42–47.

Barman, C. R., Barman, N. S., McNair, S., & Stein, M. (2003). Students' ideas about plants: Results from a national study. *Science and Children.* Retrieved December 1, 2008 from http://proquest.umi.com/pqdlink?did=3872 19071&Fmt=6&clientId=9269&RQT=309&VName=PQD

Barman, C., Stein, M., Barman, N., & McNair, S. (2002). Assessing students' ideas about plants. *Science and Children, 10*(1), 25–29.

Bell, B. F. (1981). What is a plant? Some children's ideas. *New Zealand Science Teacher, 31,* 10–14.

Bottomley, L. J., et al. (2001). Lessons learned from the implementation of a GK–12 grant outreach program. Paper presented at the 2001 American Society for Engineering Education Annual Conference, session 1692.

Brody, M. J. (1993). Student understanding of water and water resources: A review of the literature. Paper presented at the annual meeting of the American Educational Research Association, Atlanta, GA, April. (ERIC Document Reproduction Service No. ED 361 230).

Bullock, M., Gelman, R., & Baillargeon, R. (1982). The development of causal reasoning. In W. J. Friedman (ed.), *The development of psychology of time.* New York: Academic Press.

Cady, J. A., & Rearden, K. (2007). Pre-service teachers' beliefs about knowledge, mathematics and science. *School Science and Mathematics, 107*(6), 237–246.

Carmazza, A., McCloskey, M., & Green, B. (1981). Naïve beliefs in "sophisticated" subjects: Misconceptions about trajectories of objects. *Cognition, 9,* 117–123.

Carey, S. (1991). Knowledge acquisition: Enrichment or conceptual change? In S. Carey & R. Gelman (eds.), *The epigenesist of mind: Essays on biology and cognition* (pp. 257–291). Hillsdale, NJ: Lawrence Erlbaum.

Carey, S. (1985). *Conceptual change in childhood*. Cambridge, MA: MIT Press.

DeLoache, J. S., Pierroutsakos, S. L., & Uttal, D. H. (2003). The origins of pictoral competence. *Current Directions in Psychological Science, 12,* 114–118.

Duschl, R. A., Schweingruber, H.A., & Shouse, A.W. (eds.). (2006). *Taking science to school: Learning and teaching science grades K–8.* Committee on Science Learning, Kindergarten Through Eighth Grade, Board on Science Education, Center for Education, Division of Behavioral and Social Science Education. Washington, DC: National Academy Press.

Education Data Partnership. (2007). *School profile: Fiscal year 2005–2006.* Retrieved June 6, 2007, from Education Data Partnership, http://www.ed-data.k12.ca.us/.

Edwards, L., Nabors, M., & Camacho, C. (2002). The dirt on worms. *Science and Children, 40*(1), 42–46.

Erickson, G., & Tiberghien, A. (1985). Heat and temperature. In R. Driver, E. Guesne, & A. Tiberghien (eds.), *Children's ideas in science* (pp. 52–84). London, UK: Open University Press.

Espinoza, F. (2005). Experience conflicts with and undermines instruction and its legacy: Examples from two-dimensional motion. *Physics Education, 40*(3), 274–280.

Ewing, M. S., & Mills, T. J. (1994). Water literacy in college freshman: Could a cognitive imagery strategy improve understanding? *Journal of Environmental Education, 25*(4), 36–40.

Finson, K. (2002). Drawing a scientist: What we do and do not know after fifty years of drawings. *School Science and Mathematics, 102*(7), 335–345.

Fraser-Abder, P. (2004). Scientific literacy for all: Are we there yet? In P. Fraser-Abder, *Pedagogical issues in science, mathematics, and technology education.* New York: Consortium for Professional Development.

Fraser-Abder, P. (2005). Towards scientific literacy for all: An urban science teacher education model. In D. F. Berlin & A. L. White (eds.), *Collaboration for the global improvement of science and mathematics education* (pp. 141–157). Columbus, OH: International Consortium for Research in Science and Mathematics Education.

Gelman, R., & Lucariello, J. (2002). Role of learning in congnitive development. In H. Pashler (series ed.) and R. Gallistel (vol. ed.), *Steven's handbook of experimental psychology: Learning, motivation and emotion* (vol. 3, 3rd ed., pp. 395–443). New York: Wiley.

Greif, M., Nelson, D., Keil, F., & Gutierrez, F. (2006). What do children want to know about animals and artifacts? Domain specific requests for information. *Psychological Science, 17*(6), 455–459.

Harvard-Smithsonian Center for Astrophysics. (1985). *A Private Universe,* video documentary.

Hatano, G., Siegler, R. S., Richards, D. D., Inagaki, K., Stavy, R., & Wax, N. (1993). The development of biological knowledge: A multi-national study. *Cognitive Development, 8,* 47–62.

Henriques, L. (2000). Children's misconceptions about weather: A review of the literature. Retrieved from http://www.csulb.edu/~lhenriqu/NARST2000.htm.

Karplus, R., & Their, H. (1974). *SCIS teacher's handbook*. Berkeley, CA: Science Curriculum Improvement Study.

Keil, F. C. (1983). On the emergence of semantic and conceptual distinctions. *Journal of Experimental Psychology: General, 112,* 357–385.

Koch, J. (1999). *Science stories: Teachers and children as science learners*. Boston: Houghton Mifflin.

Krajcik, J., Blumenfeld, P. C., Marx, R. W., Bass, K. M., & Fredricks, J. (1998). Inquiry in project-based science classrooms: Initial attempts by middle school students. *Journal of the Learning Sciences, 7*(3/4), 313–350.

Krist, H., Fieberg, E. L., & Wilkening, F. (1993). Intuitive physics in action and judgment: The development and knowledge about projectile motion. *Journal of Experimental Psychology: Learning Memory and Cognition, 19*(4), 952–966.

Lee, O., Eichinger, D. C., Anderson, C. W., Berkheimer, G. D., & Blakeslee, T. D. (1993). Changing middle school students' conceptions of matter and molecules. *Journal of Research in Science Teaching, 30*(3), 249–270.

McDuffie, Jr., T. E. (2001). Scientists—geeks and nerds? Dispelling teachers' stereotypes of scientists. *Science and Children* (May), 16–19.

McNair, S., & Stein, M. (2001). Drawing on their understanding: Using illustrations to invoke deeper thinking about plants. Paper presented at the Association for the Education of Teachers of Science Annual Meeting, Costa Mesa, CA.

National Research Council (NRC). (1996). *National science education standards*. Washington, DC: National Academy Press.

Office of the Press Secretary. (2002). *Fact sheet: No child left behind act.* Retrieved August 8, 2007, from www.whitehouse.gov/news/releases/2002/01/20020108.html.

Osborne, R. J., & Cosgrove, M. (1983). Children's conceptions of the changes of state of water. *Journal of Research I: Science Teaching, 20*(9), 825–838.

Osborne, R. J., & Freyberg, P. (1985). *Learning in science.* London: Heinemann.

Philips, W. C. (1991). Earth science misconceptions. *Science Teacher, 58*(2), 21–23.

Poulin-Dubois, D., & Rakison, D. H. (2001). Developmental origin of the animate-inanimate distinction. *Psychological Bulletin, 127*(2), 209–228.

Rahm, J., & Charbonneau, P. (1997). Probing stereotypes through students' drawings of scientists. *American Journal of Physics, 65*(8), 774–778.

Rastovac, J. J., & Slavsky, D. B. (1986). The use of paradoxes as an instructional strategy. *Journal of College Science Teaching, 16*(2), 113–118.

Richards, D. D., & Siegler, R. S. (1984). The effects of task requirements on children's life judgments. *Child Development, 55,* 1687–1696.

Richards, D. D., & Siegler, R. S. (1986). Children's understandings of the attributes of life. *Journal of Experimental Child Psychology, 42,* 1–22.

Roth, K. (1985). *Food for plants: Teacher's guide.* Research series no. 153. East Lansing: Michigan State University, Institute of Research on Teaching. (ERIC Document Reproduction Services No. ED # 256 624).

Ryman, D. (1974). Children's understanding of the classification of living organisms. *Journal of Biological Education, 8,* 140–144.

Schoon, K. J. (1989). Misconceptions in the earth sciences: A cross-age study. Paper presented at the annual meeting of the National Associations for Research in Science Teaching, San Francisco, CA. (ERIC Document Reproduction Service No. ED 306 076).

Schoon, K. (1995). The origin and extent of alternative conceptions in the earth and space sciences: A survey of pre-service elementary teachers. *Journal of Elementary Science Education, 7*(2), 27–46.

Science Accountability Act (H.R. 35). Retrieved from http://www.govtrack. us/congress/bill.xpd?bill=h110-35.

Sere, M. G. (1985). The gaseous state. In R. Driver, E. Guesne, & A. Tiberghien (eds.), Children's ideas in science (pp. 105–123). London, UK: Open University Press.

Shanon, B. (1976). Aristotelianism, Newtownianism and the physics of the layman. *Perceptions, 5,* 241–243.

Smith, E. L., & Anderson, C. W. (1984). Plants as producers: A case study of elementary science teaching. *Journal of Research in Science Teaching, 21,* 685–698.

Sjøberg, S. (2000). *Science and scientists: The SAS-study. Cross-cultural evidence and perspectives on pupils' interests, experiences and perceptions.* University of Oslo, Oslo, Norway.

Stavy, R. (1991). Children's ideas about matter. *School Science and Mathematics, 91*(6), 240–244.

Stavy, R., & Wax, N. (1989). Children's conceptions of plants as living things. *Human Development, 62,* 767–781.

Stein, M., & McNair, S. (2002). Science drawings as a tool for analyzing conceptual understanding. Paper presented at the Association for the Education of Teachers of Science Annual Meeting, Charlotte, NC.

Stepans, J. (1985). Biology in elementary schools: Children conceptions of life. *American Biology Teacher, 47*(4), 222–225.

Stepans, J. (1994). *Targeting students' science misconceptions.* Riverview, FL: Idea Factory.

U.S. Department of Education, Office of Educational Research and Improvement, Programs for the improvement of practice, *Helping your child learn science,* August 1991.

Tunnicliffe, S. D., & Reiss, M. J. (2000). Building a model of the environment: How do children see plants? *Journal of Biological Education, 34*(4), 172–177.

Watts, M. (1983). Some alternative views of energy. *Physics Education, 18,* 213–216.

Wellman, H.M. (1990). *The child's theory of mind.* Cambridge, MA: MIT Press.

Yoachim, C. M., & Meltzoff, A. N. (2003, October). *Cause and effect in the mind of the preschool child.* Poster presented at the biennial meeting of the Cognitive Development Society, Park City, UT.

Chapter 3

Byrnes, D. A., & Kiger, G. (eds.). (2005). *Common bonds: anti-bias teaching in a diverse society.* Olney, MD: Association for Childhood Education International.

Grayson, D., & Martin, M. (2006). *Generating expectations for student achievement: An equitable approach to educational excellence.* Gray Mill, CA: Canyon Lake.

Chapter 4

Barab, S. A., & Luehmann, A. L. (2002). Building a sustainable science curriculum: Acknowledging and accommodating local adaptation. *Journal of the Learning Sciences, 10*(4), 320–351.

Bybee, R. W., Taylor, J. A., Gardner, A., Van Scotter, P., Powell, J. A., & Westbrook, A., et al. (2006). The BSCS 5E instructional model: Origins, effectiveness and applications. In *Executive Summary.* Retrieved August 8, 2007, from http://www.bscs.org/library/BSCS_5E_Model_Executive_Summary2006.pdf.

Krajcik, J., Blumenfeld, P. C., Marx, R. W., Bass, K. M., & Fredricks, J. (1998). Inquiry in project-based science classrooms: Initial attempts by middle school students. *Journal of the Learning Sciences, 7*(3/4), 313–350.

Prince, M., & Felder, R. (2007). The many faces of inductive teaching and learning. *Journal of College Science Teaching, 36*(5), 14–20.

Chapter 5

National Research Council (NCR). (1996). *National science education standards.* Washington, DC: National Academies Press.

American Association for the Advancement of Science (AAAS). (1993). *Project 2061: Benchmarks for science literacy: A tool for curriculum reform.* New York: Oxford University Press.

Harlen, W. (1999). Purposes and procedures for assessing science process skills. *Assessment in education: Principles, policy and practice, 6*(1), 129–144. Retrieved June 11, 2009, from http://www.informaworld.com/ 10.1080/09695949993044.

Harlen, W. (2001). *Primary science: Taking the plunge.* Portsmouth: Heinemann.

Harlen, W. (2005). *Teaching, learning and assessing science 5–12.* Thousand Oaks: Sage.

New York City Department of Education (NYC DOE). (2007). NYC science scope and sequence, *NYC DOE Curriculum and Professional Development: Mathematics and Science.* Retrieved June 6, 2007, from http://schools.nyc. gov/NR/rdonlyres/C17923F6-91D9-4B19-AC89-B96160F12F99/24139/ K8SSScience1.pdf.

U.S. Department of Education, Office of Educational Research and Improvement, Programs for the improvement of practice, *Helping your child learn science,* August 1991.

Chapter 6

The following are Websites and books you can use to assist in your lesson planning.

Green Curriculum

- Be a Worm Watcher, How Much Garbage, Links To Life, Will It Rot http://livablepiercecounty.org/PC/
- Teaching with Worms (A wide variety of lessons, as well as a Webquest or two) http://www.proteacher.com/cgi-bin/outsidesite.cgi?id=5319&external =http://yucky.kids.discovery.com/teachercenter/pg000066.htm&original= http://www.proteacher.com/110067.shtml&title=Worm%20World

- Worm Bin Project Unit http://commtechlab.msu.edu/Sites/letsnet/noframes/teachers/jackie/b2u1.html
- Digging Up Details on Worms: Using the Language of Science in an Inquiry Study (The lesson plan says K–2 but I think it can easily be adapted for 3–4 grade, and may even be usable as is for third grade.) http://www.readwritethink.org/lessons/lesson_view.asp?id=917
- Urban ecology waste reduction project (Includes a list of cafeteria foods that can be composted to encourage doing this for the school.) http://www.readwritethink.org/lessons/lesson_view.asp?id=917
- Inch-by-inch learning is a cinch (Not sure if this is appropriate for third-graders, but it is an interesting lesson involving the earthworm and measurement.) http://alex.state.al.us/lesson_view.php?id=14698

Kindergarten–Third-Grade Science Book Series

- *Let's Explore Science* by David Evans and Claudette Williams
- *Starting Science* by Kay Davies and Wendy Oldfield
- *Let's Read and Find Out Science* published by Harper Trophy

Fourth–Sixth-Grade Science Series

- *Eyewitness Books* published by Dorling Kindersley
- *The Magic School Bus* by Joanna Cole

Children's Science Journals

- *Ranger Rick*
- *National Geographic Kids*
- *Odyssey*
- *Your Big Backyard*
- *Kids Discover*
- *Highlights*
- *High Five*

Science Reference Books

- *The Kingfisher First Science Encyclopedia*
- *The Dorling Kindersley Science Encyclopedia*

TeachersTV.com

Chapter 7

Grant, T., & Littlejohn, G. (2005). *Teaching green: The elementary years.* Gabriola: New Society Publishers.

Leslie, C. W. (2005). *Into the field: A guide to locally focused teaching.* Great Barrington: Orion Society.

Moyer, R. H., Hackett, J. K., & Everett, S. A. (2006). *Teaching science as investigations: Modeling inquiry through learning cycle lessons.* Upper Saddle River, NJ: Prentice Hall.

Russell, H. R. (1998). *Ten-minute field trips: Using the school grounds for environmental studies.* Arlington: National Science Teachers Association.

U.S. Department of Education, Office of Educational Research and Improvement, Programs for the improvement of practice, *Helping your child learn science,* August 1991.

Education Programs

This list consists of selected education programs for use in field trips. Many of these sites also conduct virtual field trips. You should also visit the following Website for links to additional programs: http://www.yallaa.com/directory/Reference/Museums/Science

American Museum of Science and Energy—The largest exhibition of energy related exhibits in the United States. Includes live demonstrations, videos, hands-on exhibits and special events. Located in Oak Ridge, Tennessee.

The Exploratorium—Hands-on museum of science, art, and human perception in San Francisco. Site provides interactive online exhibits and exhibitions, activities, science news, and publications, general information about the museum. Located in San Francisco, California.

Great Lakes Science Center—Offers more than 340 interactive science exhibits and a six story tall Omnimax theater. Includes a visitor's guide, a calendar of events and a schedule. Located in Cleveland, Ohio.

The Imaginarium—Alaskan hands on science discovery center. Located in Anchorage.

Marian Koshland Science Museum—Features state-of-the-art exhibitions highlighting the science behind today's headlines and affecting daily lives. Plan a visit or explore the exhibits online, including virtual interactive activities. Located in Washington, DC.

National Museum of Emerging Science and Innovation—Features the global environment and frontier, life sciences and humans, technological revolution and the future, and information science. Located in Tokyo, Japan. [Japanese and English]

Natural Science Center of Greensboro—Features hands-on exhibits, zoo, and planetarium. Located in Greensboro, North Carolina.

Science Museum of Minnesota—Features dinosaurs, an Omnitheater, school programs, Mississippi Riverfront parks, and hands-on exhibits. Located in Saint Paul.

Appendix 1

American Association for the Advancement of Science (AAAS). (1993). *Project 2061: Benchmarks for science literacy: A tool for curriculum reform.* New York: Oxford University Press.

National Research Council (NCR). (1996). *National science education standards.* Washington, DC: National Academy Press.

New York City Department of Education (NYC DOE). (2007) NYC science scope and sequence, *NYC DOE Curriculum and Professional Development: Mathematics and Science.* Retrieved June 6, 2007, from http://schools.nyc. gov/NR/rdonlyres/C17923F6-91D9-4B19-AC89-B96160F12F99/24139/ K8SSScience1.pdf.

Appendix 2

American Association for the Advancement of Science. (2001). *Project 2061: Atlas of science literacy.* Washington, DC: National Science Teachers Association.

American Association for the Advancement of Science. (2007). *Project 2061: Atlas of science literacy,* vol. 2. Washington, DC: National Science Teachers Association.

Index

Note: Page numbers followed by f and t indicate figures and table respectively.

third-grade science
    content information for, 153–157
    suburban school example, 123
    urban school example, 131–132
time/timing
    in lesson plan, 129
    structuring in learning environment, 95
topic, rationale for teaching, 126–127

U
U.S. Department of Education, 36, 37
    guidelines for visits to nonformal institutions, 105
    lesson planning guidelines, 125–126
    opportunities for learning science, 134

V
variables, skills in controlling
    described, 64t
    developing, 83
variation, 92
vegetable farms, visits to, 108
virtual visits, to museums, 107, 117

visits, to nonformal science settings, 105
    aquariums, 107
    farms, 107–108
    guidelines for, 105
    museums, 107
    zoos, 105–107

W
water properties, teaching content for (grade 4), 160–161
"we teach who we are," 15
Websites
    as science teaching resources
        for all grades, 114t
        for grades 3-5, 115t–116t
    state standards on, 122
Why Board, 97
    purpose, 60
    question examples, 60
word wall, in classroom, 98

Z
zoos, visits to, 105–107
    preparing students for, 106–107

Notes

Notes